WHY ARE STUDENTS
NOT LEARNING
ON THE SCHOOL BUS?

WHY ARE STUDENTS
NOT LEARNING
ON THE SCHOOL BUS?

*The Future of Learning Outside the Classroom
in American Schools*

Keshia L. Gaines, Ph.D.

iUniverse, Inc.
Bloomington

WHY ARE STUDENTS NOT LEARNING ON THE SCHOOL BUS?
The Future of Learning Outside the Classroom in American Schools

iUniverse books may be ordered through booksellers or by contacting:

iUniverse
1663 Liberty Drive
Bloomington, IN 47403
www.iuniverse.com
1-800-Authors (1-800-288-4677)

ISBN: 978-1-4759-1604-1 (sc)
ISBN: 978-1-4759-1605-8 (ebk)

Printed in the United States of America

iUniverse rev. date: 05/08/2012

TABLE OF CONTENTS

(3.) Chapter 3: The School Bus: A Yellow Classroom

(4.) Chapter 4: The Cafeteria: Academics for Breakfast and Lunch

(5.) Chapter 5: The Bathroom: An Independent Study and Other Controversial Areas to Learn

(6.) Chapter 6: The Playground: A Fun Place to Learn

(7.) Chapter 7: Bus-stop 2 Bus-stop™ Educational Clothing for Faculty, Staff, and Students

(8.) Chapter 8: Bus-stop 2 Bus-stop™ by 2020: Political, Legal, and Ethical Concerns

PREFACE

"I am a little confused about what is happening in public schools today. After teaching in several low-performing schools in Mississippi, I noticed that students were not exposed to academic content outside the classroom very often. These non-instructional times, or missed learning opportunities, are significant factors that can influence academic achievement. Why are students not learning at the bus stop, school bus, cafeteria, bathrooms, hallways, playgrounds, and from educational clothing? From my teaching experiences, I became interested in researching how students learn outside the classroom. My Bus-stop 2 Bus-stop™ learning method continued to grow from there."

—Keshia L. Gaines, Ph.D.

About the Book

"Why are Students Not Learning on the School Bus?" provides non-traditional methods of teaching students. The author, Keshia L. Gaines, Ph.D. offers ground-breaking techniques to expand areas for learning opportunities. Research has shown that academic achievement is related to the amount of time a student is engaged in learning. Also,

x

school schedules do not highlight the non-instructional times of a student's school day. During the school day, missed learning opportunities often occur during transition times, bathroom breaks, intercom interruptions, lunch time, and many other unstructured and unplanned times. The author's new "Bus-stop 2 Bus-stop™" method is designed to replace academic down-times with unique learning opportunities for outside the classroom. (When this book refers to "learning on the school bus" or "learning outside the classroom," the author is referring to learning academic content).

Audience and Purpose

This book is designed for use in various education courses, educational leadership positions, and for general reading by anyone who is worried about the future of our children and educational systems. For entry-level students in education, this book provides insight to new ways to improve academic achievement in America. This book is also appropriate for various upper-level courses because of its research components, references, questions, and critical thinking areas. The purpose of this book is to explain the "Bus-stop 2 Bus-stop™" teaching method and to ultimately improve the current education system in America.

Goals and Features of the Book

There are three goals of this book.

1. To explain an alternative method for increasing student achievement
2. To increase school administration, teacher, and staff awareness of the new "Bus-stop 2 Bus-stop™" learning method
3. To emphasize the need for change in the unsuccessful practices of many schools in America

Also, this book can help schools improve cultural diversity, school management, and professional development. In order to meet the book's goals, this book includes discussion questions, journal activities, informative graphics, chapter research focus topics, an appendix, and a list of references. With the exception of the introduction chapter, this book has one research focus area per chapter which provides literature review-type research and background. In addition to the research component, the author has made the chapters as clear and understandable as possible. Finally, this book is a great tool to initiate focus group discussions on beneficial professional development and faculty meeting projects.

Content and Organization

"Why are Students Not Learning on the School Bus?" consists of eight chapters. The following outline highlights the eight chapters in a brief summary:

1. **Chapter 1:** Introduction to the new "Bus stop 2 Bus stop™" Learning Method—This chapter introduces the new "Bus stop 2 Bus stop™" areas for learning outside the classroom. It also gives a general overview, the author's beliefs, and a veteran teacher's perspective on learning outside the classroom.

2. **Chapter 2:** The Bus stop: The First Area for Learning—This chapter designates the bus stop as the first area for students to get exposure to academic content.

3. **Chapter 3:** The School Bus: A Yellow Classroom—Chapter 3 describes the learning opportunities which can take place on a school bus. Also, the author shares her invention "The Universal School Bus Seat Learning Pad" as one of the first devices to promote student learning on the school bus.

4. **Chapter 4**: The Cafeteria: Academics for Breakfast and Lunch—This chapter was inspired by the author's 130 page dissertation titled "A Quantitative Study of Learning in the School Cafeteria Using Educational Placemats." It offers learning opportunities for students during breakfast and lunch time. In this chapter, positive results are shown from an elementary cafeteria research study.

5. **Chapter 5:** The Bathroom: An Independent Study—and other controversial areas to learn. This chapter

discusses how to turn the school's bathroom, a commonly low-supervised area of the school, into a brief learning opportunity. Also, this chapter discusses other controversial and unique areas for students to learn.

6. **Chapter 6:** The Playground: A Fun Place to Learn— Even though, there are many hidden academic learning activities on the school playground, often times they are not maximized. The author explains incidental learning and fun ways for students to learn while playing.

7. **Chapter 7:** Bus-stop 2 Bus-stop™ Educational Clothing for Faculty, Staff, and Students—This chapter incorporates school culture, fashion, and academics on clothing as a visual aid.

8. **Chapter 8:** Bus-stop 2 Bus-stop™ by 2020: Political, Legal, and Ethical Concerns—This chapter describes the politics behind a failing American education system and the nation's struggling economy. This chapter gives financial, legal, and ethical aspects behind administering the Bus-stop 2 Bus-stop™ method.

Special Thanks

First, I would like to thank God for giving me the strength and the ability to be successful in my research endeavors. Also, I am thankful to God for allowing me to create the Bus-stop 2 Bus-stop™ learning method. I hope this method is a blessing to schools across the United States of America and other parts of the world. Also, I would like to thank my husband

and wonderful family for supporting me over the years. Last but not least, I dedicate this book to my grandmothers: Ms. Glata Monroe and the late Ms. Clemteen Edwards. Your encouragement has made a lasting impact on my life.

Also, to all crossing guards, bus drivers, security guards, cafeteria staff, janitorial and maintenance staff, secretaries, and other non-academic school personnel. You play a very important role in your school's culture. In the future, you will help students even more by increasing their academic achievement by non-traditional methods. I sincerely thank you.

Acknowledgements

The author would like to acknowledge and show appreciation to Ms. Amber Dunn for her editing services on "Why are Students Not Learning on the School Bus?" As Development Editor, Ms. Dunn has worked closely with Dr. Keshia L. Gaines to organize, edit, and revise this book. Dr. Gaines would like to say a special thank you to Ms. Amber Dunn for her assistance.

Dr. Gaines would like to thank Ms. Cyntria Patterson from Portraits-Lifetime of Memories Photography for the professional photos of Bus-stop 2 Bus-stop™ products and events.

Also, thanks to the students, staff, and administration of Little Flower School District and Center Moriches High School in Long Island, New York. It was a pleasure to tour your campuses in preparation for my book and previous research.

Bus-stop 2 Bus-stop, LLC

The Bus-stop 2 Bus-stop™ name is a trademark of Bus-stop 2 Bus-stop, LLC, a company that specializes in educational books, products, clothing, and services. All other artwork, images, and text in this book are copyrighted and belong to Dr. Keshia L. Gaines and Bus-stop 2 Bus-stop, LLC. All rights reserved.

About the Author

Keshia L. Gaines, Ph.D.

Keshia L. Gaines, Ph.D. is an internationally recognized author, educator, and inventor in the areas of education and non-traditional learning methods. Dr. Gaines has been active in public education for over 10 years. As a young educator, Gaines works hard to create innovative methods for increasing student achievement. Dr. Gaines is the founder of Bus-stop

2 Bus-stop, LLC, a company that specializes in educational books, products, clothing, and services.

The academic background of Dr. Gaines includes a Bachelors of Arts (B.A.) in English from The University of Southern Mississippi, a Masters in Education (M.Ed.) from William Carey College, and a Doctorate of Philosophy (Ph.D.) in Educational Leadership from The University of Southern Mississippi.

Gaines has worked with elementary and middle school students in several school districts in Mississippi. Her experience includes teaching both general education and special education students. Currently, she holds a MS Educator License with endorsements in Art, Elementary Education, English, Special Education, Library Media Specialist, and School Administration.

Dr. Gaines is a native of Mississippi. She enjoys traveling and spending time with her husband Kevin Gaines, a successful business manager, and close family and friends. For further information on Bus-stop 2 Bus-stop, LLC or Dr. Gaines go to www.BusStop2BusStop.com or e-mail Dr. Gaines at keshgaines@yahoo.com.

CHAPTER 1

Introduction to the Bus-stop 2 Bus-stop™ Learning Method

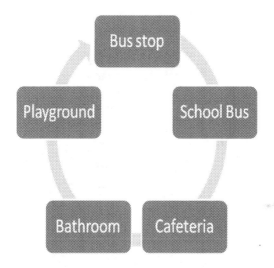

Bus-stop 2 Bus-stop™ —a learning method for increasing academic achievement by exposing students to academic content outside the classroom (areas such as the bus stop, school bus, cafeteria, bathrooms, hallways, playgrounds, other school areas, and by academic content on clothing of all students and staff members). The Bus-stop 2 Bus-stop™ Learning Method was created by Dr. Keshia L. Gaines in the Fall of 2010.

As a result of the Bus-stop 2 Bus-stop™ learning method, Dr. Gaines founded Bus-stop 2 Bus-stop, LLC, a company that specializes in educational books, clothing, products, and services.

Why are students not learning outside the classroom?

Academic achievement in America is a concern because it lacks in comparison to other countries. Since students are not meeting academic expectations in the general classroom, it is important to consider all available non-traditional areas and methods for students to learn. Learning outside the classroom can and will make a significant improvement in academic achievement in America if opportunities are introduced and implemented properly. This is heavily supported by current and past research. Researchers and practitioners have identified the need to develop alternative teaching and learning opportunities.

Bus-stop 2 Bus-stop™ Basics

The idea behind the Bus-stop 2 Bus-stop™ learning method is that students will be exposed to academic content starting at the school bus stop. Students will continue to be exposed to academic content throughout their school hours until they get dropped off at that same bus stop at the end of the school day. The name Bus-stop 2 Bus-stop™ was created because the method constantly exposes students, in many different and entertaining ways, to academic content from each "bus stop to bus stop." Since some students will not ride the school bus, this name is literal in nature. Some students walk to school, skateboard, ride a bicycle, drive (or ride in) a car, etc.

Since some of the Bus-stop 2 Bus-stop™ learning areas may not be supervised by an adult, the method serves as a means for nurturing independent learners. This method plays an important role not only in shaping the school's culture but also encouraging children to learn on their own. The corresponding research for this method is derived from brain-based learning, visual learning, repetition learning, social learning, incidental learning, and other teaching and learning aspects.

Development of the Idea

In the fall of 2010, Dr. Keshia L. Gaines began developing the Bus-stop 2 Bus-stop™ learning method. She formed the idea while trying to decorate her classroom with educational posters. After putting posters with academic content on the majority of her walls, she still had a lot of posters left. She looked over at her classroom's ugly winter-green garbage can. "Why can't the garbage can be a learning tool?" she asked herself. She took a poster with phonic sounds and vocabulary words and wrapped it around the garbage can. It was no longer just a garbage can. It was a learning opportunity and a new tool for students to be exposed to unexpected and additional academic content. Dr. Gaines could now use the garbage can in a game or as part of a quiz review. Why not?

The students look at objects that are in the classroom. Every student who used the garbage can had to look at the exterior to see how to throw in the trash. In the following months, Dr. Gaines continued to write, research, and record this unique learning method.

A Change in Thinking about Learning

In preparation for her students' state-wide testing, Dr. Gaines removed or covered all academic posters in her classroom. This is the standard procedure to meet district and state regulations. As an additional precaution, Dr. Gaines's school district sent central office personnel inspectors to the school sites to double check for visible academic content. Because of her curiosity, Dr. Gaines left the academic poster on the garbage can to see if the central office inspector would recognize the violation. Dr. Gaines placed the garbage can by the front of the classroom so it would be clearly visible to the inspector. When the central office inspector came into Dr. Gaines's classroom, she walked past the garbage can and thoroughly inspected the room for violations. Dr. Gaines kept quiet. After several minutes of examining the classroom, the inspector verified that no academic content was visible. Why did the inspector overlook the garbage can with academic content?

As the inspector exited the classroom, Dr. Gaines stopped her and pointed out the academic content on the garbage can. The inspector was shocked. After discussing the garbage can's academic purpose, the inspector stated that she was used to inspecting "traditional areas" for learning. The inspector also stated that she had never considered a garbage can as a learning tool. Dr. Gaines realized that some new, non-traditional methods for learning should be implemented into schools. Also at this point, Dr. Gaines realized that teachers, administrators, and all other staff should change their way of thinking about education. The Bus-stop 2 Bus-stop™ method continued to expand from this to include many other areas outside the classroom.

History of Time-on Task: Time Spent Learning

During the 20th century, several researchers investigated the link between instructional time and learning. These studies break down into the following categories: days in the school year, time in the school day, and instructional time. The first category, days in the school year, is considered when restructuring schools. Recently, attention has focused to increasing days in the school year to allow for more learning. If the school year, which is approximately 180 days in the United States, is lengthened, schools would use their same instructional practices for a longer amount of time. The Bus-stop 2 Bus-stop™ method will increase academic achievement with either a regular school calendar or a lengthened version.

In order to examine "time on task" in a more productive way, time in the school day should be considered. Most schools appear to have eight hours allocated to instruction. Policy governs instructional time allocation, but teachers have control over actual instructional time within their classroom. Instructional time varies amongst teachers because their classrooms vary largely in learning content and structure. For example, a new teacher may experience less "time on task" because of discipline problems and class interruptions. Academic learning time is hard to measure because of the discrepancies between when students are learning and when they are not. How can learning outside the classroom be measured for student academic achievement?

Many classrooms in America include students from diverse backgrounds. Often time students do not have a strong foundation for learning when they enter school. Prior knowledge of academic content and prerequisite skills for a lesson must be strong, or at least introduced, before a student can progress. According to Dr. Gaines's research, these basic skills can be learned in informal settings such as the bus stop, school bus, or cafeteria. Also, when students are in unstructured environments, more disciplinary problems usually arise. Disciplinary problems and poor academic achievement are very closely related.

As far as visual learning is concerned, studies show that on average there are more visual learning students than auditory learners. Also, learning has a positive correlation with repetition. Students usually do not remember a concept or lesson the first time it is introduced to them, but they eventually remember it after several repetitions. Many Bus-stop 2 Bus-stop™ areas can increase student achievement by social learning, just as businesses use advertising techniques such as billboards, television ads, or employees holding signs and or advertisements. Students can interact with the learning content without teacher or adult direction. Bus-stop 2 Bus-stop™ clothing, which includes academic content, may cause students to interact with each other about the academic content on their clothing (see chapter 7 for information on Bus-stop 2 Bus-stop™ clothing for faculty, staff and students).

Dr. Gaines's Beliefs

1. Clothing worn to school by students, teachers, staff, and administrators should serve some educational purpose.
2. Areas of the school, such as the school cafeteria, playgrounds, and bathrooms should serve an educational purpose.
3. T-shirts and other school-related clothing made for school use and wear should include educational content.
4. Students should be learning educational content at the bus stop and on the school bus.
5. School superintendents, principals, and other staff members should troubleshoot to turn non-academic times during the school day into academic learning opportunities.
6. There should be little to no educational "down-time" during the school day.
7. All classified staff should serve some sort of educational purpose. For example, the janitors should wear uniforms with educational content and also have a janitor's cart with additional educational content on it.
8. All staff members should have an introductory amount of educational administration training.

This picture shows several educational products
such as posters, clothing, cafeteria placemats, and a basketball
designed by Dr. Gaines.

Lunch with Dr. Gaines: An Informal Teacher Interview

Dr. Gaines: Alright, thank you Teacher A for allowing me to interview you about learning outside the classroom. My first question for today is "What is your perspective on learning outside the classroom during the school day?"

Teacher A: Um, my perspective is that there are many missed learning opportunities during the day. Children come to school with preconceived notions of what learning is supposed to be, and teachers do as well. We need to look at all opportunities and ways that we can reach children on different levels.

Dr. Gaines: . . . and with you being a gifted teacher and all . . . I know you work hard with your gifted students. How much time would you be willing to put into learning about teaching outside the classroom?

Teacher A: Well, all teachers are required to participate in professional development and I am willing to participate in any workshop, quarter, or semester work. I think any teacher would be willing to participate too.

Dr. Gaines: Do you know of any missed learning opportunities that you can identify during your student's schedule? Not something that is just your fault, but a time when they are not receiving academic content.

Teacher A: Oh, yeah . . . . students just sit around and socialize in the cafeteria and at the end of the school day. You know, I participated in a gifted workshop where a director of gifted ed. in a school engaged children in learning in the cafeteria. It was a question and answer period of what every third grader should know. It was fun, like trivia questions. It was a fun time! Children would go home and try to research the subject. "Who's the sixteenth president of the United States?" "What are the oceans of the world?"

Dr. Gaines: . . . right, right, that's a good idea.

Dr. Gaines: In your opinion, how many minutes of a student's daily schedule are non-instructional?

Teacher A: Oooh, well I don't have a clear idea since I am specialized and I do a pull-out program, but I would assume-being from my former background as a regular classroom teacher . . . at least an hour to an hour and a half. I'm just making a good guess.

Dr. Gaines: Okay. Uum, what do you think about a program or workshop that is used to explain or utilize missed learning opportunities? . . . the non-instructional times in a student's day. Do you think a program, an instructional program, would be able to help?

Teacher A: . . . sure . . .

Dr. Gaines: Do you think it will be able to help the teachers?

Teacher A: I think it will help gain knowledge on how to make students learn better. I'm sure all teachers are open to that idea.

Dr. Gaines: Okay . . . uum . . . well having said that, could providing instructional review during this missed learning opportunity increase academic achievement?

Teacher A: Yes, I think so. I think if we expose students to a situation at least four times, it becomes a learning opportunity. Children learn by repetition.

Dr. Gaines: Okay . . . well, we said teachers, but what about the administrators and other staff members. How do you think they will view an opportunity to increase learning opportunities?

Teacher A: Well, I don't really know. I think every administration in every district has a different set of goals or objectives . . . but educators should use every opportunity they can to enhance student learning.

Dr. Gaines: okay . . . uum . . . well, how would the students view the loss of their down-times or transition times? In the hallways, cafeteria, other places where they are not receiving instruction. How do you think the students will react with those times being replaced by a learning opportunity?

Teacher A: I think it's all in the way that it is delivered. The delivery system is the key to the student "buying-in" to the idea if it is presented in a fun, interesting, very innovative way. They are learning something everyday, either positive or negative . . . so why not take this opportunity. I think they would be very receptive.

Dr. Gaines: Okay . . . uum . . . what about stakeholders? Do you think stakeholders would be willing to play the part in increasing instructional time?

Teacher A: Oh, I think that they could be a key component to working with children. Teachers and administrators are only going to be available to work with students at certain times. The other stakeholders could be on the school site when a teacher is not available. It would be great to have volunteers administer the system or to provide these opportunities.

Dr. Gaines: Okay . . . when we start talking about increasing student achievement, some people think about money. I mean, the budget is tight. The money

	is funny. Do you think that increasing these learning opportunities equates to more money being spent?
Teacher A:	. . . No . . .
Dr. Gaines:	What do you think about this issue?
Teacher A:	I think it has been proven in the past that you can throw money at education all day long, and it will not affect student achievement as much as committed educators and a delivery system that makes learning fun and makes it . . . uuh . . . hands-on. The child has to take ownership of their learning. They have to become a part of the system, not just a receiver of it. They have to have ownership in their own education. It's not about money. It's about innovation and making learning fun.
Dr. Gaines:	Okay (Pause)
Teacher A:	Oh, and to piggy back on that, children have TV's, video games, etc. nowadays. They are used to being entertained. They are so used to being a receiver. They need to be a part of the whole process. Their success is the success of their school.
Dr. Gaines:	. . . so . . . not just changing the amount of learning opportunities, but trying to change the culture of students so they will take responsibility for their own education?
Teacher A:	Exactly . . . exactly
Dr. Gaines:	. . . right . . . okay . . .
Teacher A:	. . . to light that fire and desire for them . . . to acquire knowledge and be personally responsible for their own achievement.

Dr. Gaines: Well . . . I know, Teacher A, we've had lunch a few times . . . and we have had time to trouble-shoot and identify missed learning opportunities within the school.

Teacher A: . . . yeah . . .

Dr. Gaines: What do you think about learning outside the classroom as far as cognitive learning or brain-based learning? Could this be one of the main focuses or problems with education?

Teacher A: I think that's it for sure! I do. I totally agree with that. I think we have so many opportunities that children could be engaged in some type of learning activity, and they are not even aware of it.

Dr. Gaines: . . . right . . .

Teacher A: . . . and you see these kids . . . they know every word to every popular song on the radio. So why can't they know the continents or the multiplication facts?

Dr. Gaines: . . . right . . . you're right . . .

Teacher A: . . . and we are failing in math because they do not have the basic computation skills they need to know. They cannot retain them.

Dr. Gaines: . . . . yeah . . .

Teacher A: . . . and why can they not retain them?

Dr. Gaines: (silence)

Teacher A: They are not practiced at home. Our cultures are so diverse now. The parents may be separated or working. To make up for this, we could provide extra learning opportunities in out-of the-box areas like the school cafeteria.

Dr. Gaines: . . . right, right.

Teacher A: If they had some type of fun while they are eating, maybe a catchy tune, they would pick it up . . . they will pick it up. No one says they have to learn all the words to a song. They just pick it up.

Dr. Gaines: . . . right . . . right.

Teacher A: . . . yep . . .

Dr. Gaines: . . . and even the music business uses repetition. You turn on the radio and you say you don't like a song at first. But after they play it over and over again . . . in traffic, etc., you are getting that repetition—and that is the key.

Teacher A: . . . they do . . . they do . . .

Dr. Gaines: yeah . . . and I even noticed the playground. Kickball. They kick the ball, run around the bases and that's it. Could even things like that be a learning opportunity?

Teacher A: Oh, I think so . . . very much so. I think the P.E. area could present the game with learning in it. Geometry "You are going in a triangle" That is an opportunity. They could learn vocabulary words in the P.E. department. You could have them posted . . . like you say . . .

Dr. Gaines: . . . . right, right . . .

Teacher A: . . . on the bases . . . First base is a square. "First" Second base. Those numbers and relationships. I see there are all types of opportunities. This could be for the younger children and then it could progress to high school level.

Dr. Gaines: Well, now since we mention P.E., you can do it with any other elective class like music, library, and other things.

Teacher A: . . . unh, hunh . . .

Dr. Gaines: I designed my educational clothing line so that teachers, students, and others can be exposed to visual learning opportunities.

Teacher A: . . . unh, hunh . . .

Dr. Gaines: I mean, the kids stare at teachers all day. They are getting that visual . . . that repetition. And if they stare at our clothes that says 2+2, maybe one day it will be 4!

Dr. Gaines: (laughing)

Teacher A: (laughing) . . . well, maybe . . .

Dr. Gaines: (laughing continued) Well, we hope so.

Teacher A: Like you say, every avenue, every time you are engaged, you are learning something.

Dr. Gaines: . . . you're right . . .

Teacher A: In our district, we have a time at the end of the day where students sit in line, kindergarten through sixth grade. They sit on the floor completely quiet. That 30 minutes could be the most fun learning time of their day. You have undivided attention there.

Dr. Gaines: . . . right . . . . right . . . .

Teacher A: It could be an interactive fun time, math facts, or maybe a story time.

Dr. Gaines: . . . oh, sure . . .

Teacher A: They couldn't wait to get back to answer the trivia question or hear the ending of a good children's story.

Dr. Gaines: . . . . oh, and I agree with you. For 30 minutes, I observe students waiting for their parents at the end of the school day. The children are just sitting there.

Teacher A: . . . . un . . . hunh . . . .

Dr. Gaines: I figure as long as children are on school property, a learning opportunity should be present. That's just my philosophy. I am eager to expose my learning techniques to schools in the United States.

Teacher A: Well, Dr. Gaines, I wish you much success in your plans for transforming American schools.

Discussion Questions for Chapter 1

1. What are some current downfalls of America's education system?

2. How do you think America's public and private school systems will benefit from the Bus-stop 2 Bus-stop™ learning method?

3. In your opinion, do American students have too much "down time" (non-instructional time) during the school day? And why?

4. What are the main areas for learning with the Bus-stop 2 Bus-stop™ method?

5. How is Bus-stop 2 Bus-stop™ different from previous learning methods in America?

Bus-stop 2 Bus-stop™ Journal Activity

Interview a retired teacher. Ask about their school's atmosphere when he or she began teaching. Explain the Bus-stop 2 Bus-stop™ learning method to the retired teacher and write a one paragraph summary about their personal perspective.

CHAPTER 2

The Bus Stop: The First Area for Learning

Why are students not learning at the bus stop?

The first area for academic exposure with the Bus-stop 2 Bus-stop™ learning method is the bus stop. Traditionally, students in America stand at the bus stop for a varied amount of time (approximately 10-15 minutes) waiting for the school bus. This time can be turned into a learning opportunity if the bus stop bench and surrounding areas included academic content similar to the advertisements that businesses use to sell their services and products. Schools can also use in-ground signage and folders allocated for students to study at the bus stop. Since students will learn independently at the bus stop, teachers could provide an incentive or reward for students that bring their folders on a daily basis. Similarly, walking and car-riding students can benefit from the study folder also. Since all students do not ride the school bus, some student's first Bus-stop 2 Bus-stop™ experience may be the school's sidewalk or hallways.

The Classroom is Too Late

Dr. Gaines believes that the classroom should not be the first area to expose students to learning. "The classroom is too late," Gaines explains. "Students have already spent up to one hour of non-instructional time." This includes standing at the school bus, eating breakfast in the cafeteria, and unstructured socializing with peers. Gaines points out that the morning is the best time for students to learn because they are well-rested and alert. "If students started getting exposure to academic content at the bus stop, this would greatly reduce educational down time," Gaines adds.

Another one of the main focuses with the Bus-stop 2 Bus-stop™ method is increasing the actual learning time of students. When students stand at the bus stop, they can be exposed to academic content while waiting for the bus. Since academic "down time" is a big concern, this chapter will focus on how increasing academic learning time will increase academic achievement.

Chapter 2 Research Focus: Academic Learning Time and Academic Achievement

The amount of time students spend learning has continued to be a very important topic for schools, teachers, and other stakeholders in education. Throughout the United States, researchers are testing the hypothesis that increased learning time enhances performance and the quality of education (Phelps, 2010). The interest in increasing learning time is motivated by the belief that the current system was constructed to accommodate farms and industries. Some believe that the 180-day calendar does not meet the needs of twenty-first century students. The system does not allow teachers and students to cover enough information to increase academic performance (McMurrer, 2008).

How could learning at the bus stop help academic achievement?

Many aspects of education have changed over the years, therefore, schools should accommodate these changes. Even though the curriculum changes often, there have been very minimal changes in terms of time allocated for learning curriculum. There are also many advancements of technology in the education system which creates more demands for educators, in terms of time. Increasing learning time means adding to the length of a school day, week, or year (Al-Balhan, 2007). The objective of additional time is restructuring the school for greater focus on academic achievement. Programs and activities that increase learning time are very effective because they give students more opportunities to learn. It is believed that 30 percent additional learning time could greatly change the academic achievement of a student (McMurrer, 2008).

This topic has prompted a lot of research to investigate whether there will be a positive or negative effect of increasing academic learning time. Interest in this issue can be traced back to the work of John Carroll in his original model of learning in school (Carroll, 1963). The theory was based on the argument that "learning is a function of time engaged relative to time needed for learning" (Gettinger & Seibert, n.d, p. 1). One of the most popular investigations of the relationship between time spent in learning and academic achievement was the Beginning Teacher Evaluation Study (BTES) by Denham (1980). The most important finding from this research was that Academic Learning Time (ALT) is a major factor in academic achievement. Among the various factors that determine academic achievement, Academic Learning Time has been given special importance by policy-makers in education due to the significance of the BTES results. Elements of ALT are seen as something that educators can control. Studies on effective teaching and learning have recognized evidence-based practices that are aimed at maximizing learning time for all learners. Since time is a crucial factor in learning, there are best practices that have been identified by teachers, for evaluating, extending and enhancing Academic Learning Time (McMurrer, 2008). Some of these are ensuring time-on-task, effective transitioning periods, and fewer disruptions in the classroom.

Phelps (2010) suggested that even without the evidence from academic research, it is apparent that the more time spent on learning, the more learning takes place. Likewise, academic studies have confirmed that a positive correlation exists between time and academic achievement. However, this relationship is quite complicated (Phelps, 2010). This is because simply increasing learning time will not automatically result in increased academic achievement. Unfortunately not all academic time allocated for instruction is actually spent on instruction. For example, a one hour class may include ten minutes of distributing worksheets and five minutes of student interruptions leaving only 45 minutes for instruction (Tripp, Basye, Jones, & Tripp, 2008).

The importance of engaged time is revealed by the large volume of research that highlights the need to increase student engagement. Al-Balhan (2007) suggested that students are often not effectively engaged in a task, or are not utilizing the class or learning time, as productively as required. This study identified the teacher as important to make sure tasks were monitored and that learners were stimulated. Al-Balhan suggested that the teacher should also encourage students to use their abilities and skills in order to be productive. For the engagement time to be effective, it is important for the learner to participate in effective tasks and at a high degree of success (Al-Balhan, 2007).

Understanding Academic Learning Time and Student Success

Before asking the "wh questions" (who, what, where, when, why) about academic learning time at the bus-stop, consider the social, cultural, and political aspects which affect a student's success. Tripp, Basye, Jones, & Tripp (2008) defined Academic Learning Time as the amount and quality of time a learner spends while performing appropriate academic tasks with a high rate of success. It is the period when the instructional activity is clearly aligned with the readiness of the student to learn. There are four main variables that contribute to Academic Learning Time. These four variables are: allocated time, time utilized for instruction, engaged time, and academic success and engagement. The "process by which allocated time is converted to productive learning time depends on school procedures, classroom practices, and individual differences between students" (Baker, Fabrega, Galindo & Mishook, 2005, p. 312).

Learning Variations Across Classrooms and Schools

Allocated time refers to the amount of time that educators plan to utilize for instructional purposes. Scales, Roehlkepartain, Neal, Kielsmeier, & Benson (2006) suggested that allocated time is the in-class opportunity for the learners to be involved in the learning process. Studies have recorded significant variation across classrooms and schools in the amount of allocated time. Despite the differences, teachers often allocate homework for additional learning time. For example, one teacher may allocate 30 minutes worth of homework, while another teacher only allocates 10 minutes worth. Variations in homework assignments and class structures means that the total allocated time for students will vary greatly. The differences between the allocated time and the time required for learning varies with students inside the classroom. Some believe that educators need to analyze learning differences in order to determine the amount of time required for each student to master the content. Students learn at different rates and the allocated time must reflect this (Scales, Roehlkepartain, Neal, Kielsmeier, & Benson, 2006).

Instructional time refers to the proportion of the time allocated that is actually used in instructional activities. Researchers have constantly revealed the fact that a limited percentage of allocated time is spent for instructional purposes (Scales et al., 2006). This percentage is normally between 50 and 60 percent. There are various activities that take place in classrooms that may affect the amount of time that is allocated for instructional purposes. To get a true estimate of instructional time, a researcher must deduct activities and other distractions. The amount of time that is spent on other activities besides instructional ones is referred to as "lost time." Hollowood carried out direct observations on eight elementary classes (Gettinger & Seibert, n.d). He identified six causes of lost instructional time—learner interruptions; teacher interruptions; people visiting the class while in session; loudspeaker announcements; transitions, and other sources (Huyvaert, 1998).

What is Student Engagement?

Engagement time is the percentage of instructional time the students are engaged in learning (Huyvaert, 1998). This proof for engagement rate is paying attention, finishing written assignments, or working with the classmates on assignments (Kosanovich, Weinstein, & Goldman, 2009). This time comprises of inactive responding (where the learners are inactively attending to a presentation or activity) and active responding (where learners are actively responding to a presentation or activity). In a class where students are provided with equal opportunities to learn, differences exist in their personal levels of engagement or participation. Pressley et al (1998) carried out observations in nine first-grade classes for educators who had been recognized as exceptional as far as literacy instruction is concerned. They discovered that despite the fact that most learners were engaged 80-90 percent of the time, in a number of classrooms engagement level was as low as 50 percent (cited in Gettinger & Seibert, n.d).

Engagement time is a significant variable in student learning. Nystrand and Gamaron (1991) have identified two kinds of learner engagement (cited in Huyvaert, 1998). They are called procedural engagement and substantive engagement. The first type, procedural engagement, comprises of observable behavior such as paying attention while the teacher is instructing and finishing assignments. When scholars talk of engagement time, they are actually referring to procedural engagement. The second type of engagement, learner engagement, engages an individual to become receptive of the academic content. Even though procedural engagement is associated with academic achievement, learning is not achievable without substantive engagement (Nystrand & Gamaron, 1991). The difference between the two is significant in understanding Academic Learning Time (Al-Balhan, 2007). Academic Learning Time is dependent not only on a specific learner's procedural engagement with their class work, but also on the characteristic and quality of their class work. When learners are involved in non-essential activities, Academic Learning Time is minimized because the students are not fully engaged. It is not beneficial for learners to use time for learning tasks that are too simple, too hard, or uninteresting. Academic achievement and productivity include the fourth significant factor of Academic Learning Time, which is the rate of academic success and engagement (Huyvaert, 1998).

The Higher the Engagement, The Higher the Achievement

The *rate of achievement and productivity* represents the proportion of engaged time, where the learners are involved in doing productive and pertinent instructional activities. These activities offer a balance of medium and high success. This happens when more tasks are targeted at high levels of success and achievement. Studies reveal that students achieve more from academic learning time when they achieve a comparatively high level of engagement. Optimizing academic achievement and productivity are dependent on the instructor to match learning activities to personal student needs, abilities, and interests (Kosanovich, Weinstein & Goldman, 2009).

According to Kosanovich, Weinstein and Goldman (2009), the percentage of *engaged time* affects academic achievement more positively than the other types of time. In other words, engaged learning time determines academic achievement. Academic Learning Time is multi-faceted. Best practices necessitate that instructors optimize instructional time and minimize lost time so that learners may have high engagement rates. When teachers allocate more time and ensure that this time is used effectively, it positively affects academic performance (Huyvaert, 1998).

Bus-stop 2 Bus-stop™ Learning at the Bus Stop

In the book, *Time is of the Essence by* Huyvaert, (1998) one of the identified ways of increasing Academic Learning

Time is increasing the scheduled time. Even though there are many ways ALT can be increased, increasing scheduled time can prove to be effective. This can be achieved by increasing the time spent on student learning by affecting the school day or the school year. According to Rock and Thread (2009), an increase of scheduled time to learn academic content can help to ensure improved academic performance, if the extra time is allocated and utilized effectively (Rock & Thread, 2009).

A school day consists of the beginning of school (when students arrive at school) until school ends (when students leave school). In other words, a school day is "from bus-stop to bus-stop" for bus riding students. There are various activities that take place during the school day. Each school day has a specific number of classes that last a specific period of time (Scales et al., 2006). There are also scheduled breaks that are used for eating, bathroom, and engaging in physical exercises; such as sports and games. Schools include activities that are aimed at awakening and focusing the attention of the learner on learning activities (Rock & Thread, 2009).

Kirkland, Camp and Manning (2008) suggested that the United States government does not require a specific number of school days in a year. Each state sets the length of the school year. The U.S. Department of Education estimates that schools in the United States spend an average of 180 days in a school year (Fisher, 2009). This estimate includes both private and public schools. It also includes elementary and secondary education levels. A report, by the Education Commission of the States in 2004, showed the requirements of each school year per state. Thirty of the states required 180 school days in every school year. There were two states with longer than 180 school days and 11 with less than 180 days (Baker, Fabrega,

Galindo & Mishook, 2005). Minnesota is one of few states that do not require a particular number of school days per year. Many nations in other parts of the world have more school days per year when compared to the United States. There are some nations that have as many as 220 school days per school year (Kirkland, Camp & Manning, 2008).

In the past decade, there have been minor changes in the average number of school days per school year. For most schools, the school days occur during a 9 to 10 month period. This period is mostly between "early fall and early summer" (Kirkland, Camp & Manning, 2008, p. 123). Approximately 86 percent of conventional public schools use this format when allocating their school days. Overall, there have been slight changes in the structure of the school day and school year. The average conventional public school added approximately four minutes, and average private school added approximately six minutes. Schools have also added days in their school year (Rock & Thread, 2009). On average, learners in conventional secondary schools use approximately six hours and 45 minutes in every school day for structured learning. The time spent in school is a little bit less for elementary students; it is approximately six hours and 36 minutes. The time is more for middle and secondary school learners approximated at 6 hours and 50 minutes. Conventional public schools tend to have shorter school days when compared to equivalent private schools (Fisher, 2009).

Let's Make up for Summer Vacation

The summer vacation is a common term in the United States education system. It is a vacation during the summer period between school years, when most schools are not in session. During this time, the students and teachers are out of school from six to twelve weeks. This period varies widely within states and districts. There has been much support as well as criticism for this holiday. Supporters of summer vacation have argued that students were over-stimulated in the system and needed 48 weeks in a school year (Kirkland, Camp & Manning, 2008). Supporters of summer vacation state that the few weeks offered by the vacation are to relax. Some of the opponents of the long vacation have argued that schools in the United States spend fewer days per school year in school as compared to schools in other countries. Researchers in the United States education systems have stated that having such a long vacation puts American students at a disadvantage because in other competitive countries students do not have such a long time for vacation (Kirkland, Camp, & Manning, 2008).

There have been requests to re-shape the structure of school day and school year to increase learning time and academic performance. Herbert (2009) has been quoted in the New York Times pointing out the major flaws of America's public education system; such as the drop-out rate and student illiteracy percentages. Herbert represents many of the supporters of the movement to change the education system in the United States to increase learning time for improved academic performance. Goldberg (2011) argued that increased learning time means using a longer school day, week, or year to significantly increase the total number of school hours for learning time. The main areas for learning are as follows:

(a) instruction in core academic subjects, including English, reading or language arts, mathematics, science, foreign languages, civics and government, economics, arts, history, and geography.

(b) instruction in other subjects and enrichment activities that contribute to a well-rounded education, for example, physical education, service learning, experiential and work-based learning opportunities that are provided by partnering (as appropriate) with other organizations.

(c) and teacher collaboration, planning, and engagement in professional development within and across grades and subjects (Goldberg, 2011).

Changing the shape of a school day and a school year has been advocated by many different education stakeholders. Rock and Thread (2009) recommended that increasing the length of a school day and year seems to be a solution to increasing academic achievement. This is supported by the argument that the current structure of school day and year is not conducive to improving academic achievement. Sometimes, when students are out of school for summer vacation, parents feel compelled to give their children learning activities so they will not regress. Some parents even enroll their children in private summer schools. This might not have to happen if the structure of the school year was reshaped to increase learning time in school (Rock & Thread, 2009).

A Student's Favorite Part of the School Day—Learning at the Bus Stop

In the article, *Learning outside the Classroom: What Can Be Done in Lesson Time?*, Wood and Walker (2007) argued that learning is not confined to classrooms. This means that students do not only learn when they are seated in the classroom and there is a teacher instructing them. Many times, the best opportunities for learning occur outside the classroom. Just as adults continue to learn more every day of their lives, children are learning constantly as well. The primary focus should be learning academic content instead of non-academic material. Whether before school, during meals in school, after school, or even during the weekend, there are great avenues to encourage innovative ways of learning outside the classroom. Often times, lunch or recess is a student's favorite part of the school day. A very small percentage of students will admit to enjoying instruction time in the classroom. As a result, the education system should be structured in such a way that every experience during the school day is an opportunity for learning.

The learning process can take place both with student awareness and without student awareness. Wood and Walker (2007) called this *incidental learning or non-conscious learning*. Through student awareness it can happen as a student is standing at the bus stop and recognizes something that the teacher has taught in the classroom. Without student awareness it may happen when a student encounters something during lunch or recess and remembers it in class when the teacher introduces the topic. The student may not be aware that such a topic exists in his or her subject when he or she learns it incidentally (Wood & Walker, 2007). Learning outside the classroom, in areas like at the bus stop or school playground, creates an engaging environment that encourages children to reach their full potential. These avenues for learning are especially effective due to the fact that students learn more when they do things they enjoy. Areas outside the classroom can provide fun and interesting learning activities (Wood & Walker, 2007). Additionally, when students learn through real life experiences, they are in a much better position to remember the academic content. There are many different ways that may help improve our current education system. The most important focus is to structure the students' time into academic learning opportunities.

Discussion Questions for Chapter 2

1. What are some ways local schools could implement the Bus-stop 2 Bus-stop™ method of learning at the bus-stop?
2. How are city bus stops and school bus stops alike and different?
3. What recent research findings about teaching and learning does the Bus-stop 2 Bus-stop™ method support?
4. Why does Dr. Gaines believe students should be exposed to academic content at the school bus stop?
5. In your opinion, what age group of students would be most successful from learning at the bus stop?

Bus-stop 2 Bus-stop™ Journal Activity

Draw a picture of five students standing at the bus stop. Include a bus stop bench and some in-ground signs that include academic content. Write 5 sentences that describe your scene.

CHAPTER 3

The School Bus: A Yellow Classroom

Why are students not learning on the school bus?

For many years students have been transported to and from school by school buses. School districts spend millions of dollars nationally to provide a variety of transportation for students. However, these funds spent on student transportation could also provide an educational benefit if students were exposed to academic content while on the buses.

The interior and exterior of a traditional school bus in America is basically the same in all parts of the country. Most school busses have a bright yellow exterior and a uniform interior, which usually includes the bus-driver's area and large bus seats for the students. The large backs of the bus seats are a perfect opportunity to provide educational content. Also, television screens could be mounted on school buses, if funds were available. Learning programs should play while a student is riding to and from school. This would greatly increase academic exposure. The academic content should reflect the types of students on that bus route. For example, a bus route with high school students would display high school content on the television screens, while middle or elementary students would display materials tailored to their specific learning levels.

An inexpensive way to use this method is to attach small posters or cards, with academic content, above each window on the interior of the bus. This could serve an academic purpose as well as reminding students of their assigned seats. Another inexpensive way to add academic opportunities on the school bus is to add an audio system, which can play catchy songs with academic content. This auditory learning method is better than not providing a learning opportunity at all, but it will have a lesser impact than a visual learning system or a visual learning system with audio.

In considering the larger context of academic content, school buses should include academic content on the exterior of the bus, just as city buses advertise on their exteriors. Specific bus routes could have assigned bus seats with specific study content and study partners. The school could hire a traveling bus tutor to assist students while learning on the school bus. The school bus has been an area of missed learning opportunity for years!

New Invention by Dr. Gaines:
The Universal School Bus Seat Learning Pad

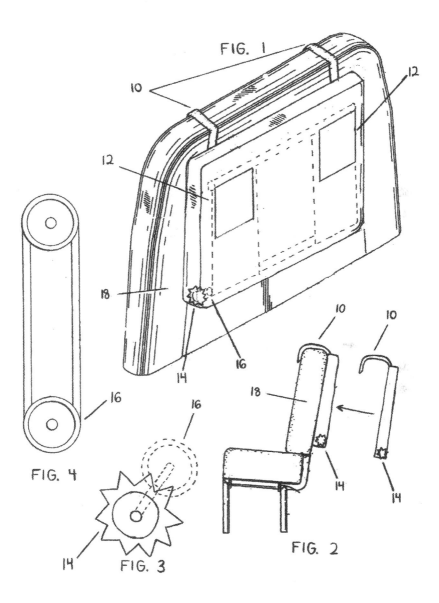

FIG. 1

FIG. 4

FIG. 3

FIG. 2

Overview of Invention

Purpose of Invention

The purpose of this invention is to provide a learning opportunity for children riding the school bus. Ultimately, this learning opportunity will increase overall academic achievement because children can learn from non-traditional areas. This invention gives students an additional opportunity to learn during the school day.

Brief Description of Invention

This invention is a learning system which is mounted on the back of a school bus seat for educational purposes. In addition, the invention includes transparent windows for viewing the academic content within. The front surface allows the inserting of various posters which display academic content. The interior of the learning system consists of a pulley with academic content on the pulley belt. The posters and academic content on the pulley belts can be interchanged as needed to meet the academic levels of the children on a specific bus route. Another version of this invention includes an electronic pad with touch screen electronic games and learning activities.

Description of the problems solved by the invention

This invention will increase the academic achievement of students on the school bus. Since many students in America are not meeting their academic expectations (and potential) in the general classroom, it is important to consider all methods and areas for students to learn. The school bus will be an additional area for learning that will help students increase academic achievement. Also, The Universal School Bus Seat Learning Pad will provide something positive (and educational) for students to do while riding the school bus.

How the invention is an improvement over existing technology

This invention is the first known learning system designed especially for the back of a school bus seat. Other electronic and non-electronic products are designed for classroom and in-school use only. Many learning systems require electricity or battery use, but this invention works without additional energy sources. Students simply turn the knob on the learning pad to view the academic content on the pulley belt.

Groups of people that would use the invention

The target groups may include all school districts (public schools and private schools), daycares, summer camp programs, church groups, non-profit organizations, and others that transport children or young adults by a school bus.

Benefits to users of the Invention

This invention will provide many opportunities for students to learn while riding the school bus. This invention will also help users learn important educational content and improve on their report cards, classroom performance, and quizzes/tests. The Universal School Bus Seat Learning Pad will provide something positive and educational for students to entertain themselves with while riding the school bus.

Descriptions of the Illustrations

Figure 1 is an enlarged side angle view of the Universal School Bus Seat Learning Pad attached to the back of a typical school bus seat.

Figure 2 shows the left side view of the invention attached to the back of a typical school bus seat. Also, Figure 2 shows a left side view of the invention by itself.

Figure 3 shows the turning mechanism of the pulley belt in greater detail.

Figure 4 is a side view of a pulley belt used in the invention. Many different types of academic content can be attached to the pulley belt; and the academic content will be easily interchanged.

Reference numeral and Descriptive name for part

    10 - Curved attachment hooks

    12 - Transparent viewing windows

    14 - Turning knob for pulley belt

    16 - Pulley belt wheel with a grooved rim

    18 - Back rest of a school bus seat (not part of this invention-for visual demonstration only)

The invention operates by students turning a knob which then turns a pulley belt which displays academic content. The passenger may view the content on the enclosed pulley belt through the transparent windows. Since this version of the invention is manually operated, the passenger may turn the knob at his or her desired pace.

Unique features of Invention

1. Interchangeable pulley belt with academic content
2. Manually operated
3. Universal for mounting on the back of any size school bus seat

Alternative Versions of this Invention

1. Solar powered pulley belts which includes a solar panel on the top of the school bus
2. Battery powered pulley belts
3. Various sizes, shapes, and materials to make invention
4. Hooks that allow the invention to be screwed or bolted to the bus seat
5. An electronic pad version with touch screen electronic games and learning activities.

Chapter 3 Research Focus:
Vygotsky's Social Learning Theory

In addition to the author's beliefs about learning on the school bus, this learning area includes a social learning component. When students ride the school bus, they talk and socially interact with their peers. If a learning support, such as Dr. Gaines's learning pad invention, educational posters, or visual aides are used, students can learn through social learning. These are called scaffolds, or temporary learning supports, and can be adjusted once a student learns the content. As detailed below, Vygotsky's social learning theory can work with or without teacher guidance. As long as students have a More Knowledgeable Other (MKO), they can learn academic content through social interaction. A More Knowledgeable Other is any person that has more knowledge on a subject than the person being taught.

Lev Semenovich Vygotsky (1896-1934), a Russian theorist, is best known for his research on social learning. Vygotsky's social learning theory involves cultural and social contexts of learning and how it shapes development. He believed "every function in the child's cultural development appears twice: first, on the social level, and later, on the individual level; first, between people (interpsychological) and then inside the child (intrapsychological)" (Vygotsky & Cole, 1978, p. 57). These social interactions, which are influenced by personal, social, and cultural factors, work together for learning to take place. In short, this theory explains how learning and consciousness are the results of socialization.

According to Daniels (2001), Vygotsky's theory breaks down into three categories: the Zone of Proximal Development (ZPD), social learning preceding development, and More Knowledgeable Others (MKO). The Zone of Proximal Development refers to tasks a child cannot complete alone, but can complete with the assistance of an adult (Daniels, 2001). In his own words, ZPD, is "the distance between the actual developmental level as determined by independent problem solving and the level of potential development as determined through problem solving under adult guidance or in collaboration with more capable peers" (Vygotsky & Cole, 1978, p. 86).

Vygotsky believed that this method encourages a child to achieve a higher level of achievement than usual. With the child exposed to challenges of a greater difficulty, he or she is able to engage in dialogue with self or others, such as the teacher. Dolya (2010) agrees that this external monologue is internalized as thought. Children can perform at higher levels with help from a More Knowledgeable Other. This can be any person that can help the child academically (Dolya, 2010). The interpretation of ZPD caused ongoing tensions between researchers Valsiner and Gergen and the idea of others. Within the two levels of ZPD, the top represents when the student cannot function without assistance and the bottom level represents when the student can function independently. Dolya (2010) also agrees with Vygotsky in that the teacher and others play an important role in student learning. The Zone of Proximal Development is described as an apprenticeship (Schunk, 2007, p. 248). Others term the participants as more able and less able (Luckin, 1999).

Vygotsky stated "that in order to understand the individual, one must first understand the social relations in which the individual exists" (Wertsch, 1985, p. 15). According to Vygotsky, socialization effects how humans think. His insight was that the social context of a child is critical to knowledge acquisition and mind processing. Areas such as a child's school building, housing community, and other surroundings greatly affect the child's thought patterns. Also, Bodrova and Leong (1996) echoed Vygotsky's idea of cognition in an external context.

Temporary Learning Supports AKA Scaffolds

Alongside Vygotsky's concept of Zone of Proximal Development, he invented a concept called *scaffolding*. Vygotsky defined a scaffold as the "role of teachers and others in supporting the learner's development and providing support structures to get to that next stage or level" (Raymond, 2000, p. 176). Basically, scaffolding involves a More Knowledgeable Other (MKO) providing some sort of support, or "scaffold" to help the learner. Shortly after being introduced to the scaffold, the learner may begin to use prior knowledge to understand new content. Scaffolding also involves introducing information on the higher end of the learner's ZPD (Olson & Pratt, 2000). Bransford, Brown, & Cocking (2000) explains scaffolding as the MKO helping the learner reach the high end of the ZPD.

Since scaffolds are temporary in nature, the MKO can withdraw them when the learner's capabilities increase. The goal of using scaffolding is for the learner to master the academic content individually (Hartman, 2002). When the learner's knowledge increases, the teacher can reduce the scaffolds. A quote by Vygotsky in Raymond (2000) says that "the system of knowledge itself becomes part of the scaffold or social support for the new learning" (Raymond, 2000, p.176). Examples of scaffolds include models and prompts of various types for learner assistance (Hartman, 2002). After the MKO introduces the scaffolds to the learner, he or she may engage in social learning with others (Hartman, 2002). With scaffolds like The Universal School Bus Seat Learning Pad, learners of various academic levels can interact with each other.

McKenzie (1999) agrees that scaffolding can be used to engage students in learning because it provides a tool for students to organize and focus. In "Scaffolding for Success" McKenzie (1999) describes scaffolding into eight characteristics. These characteristics describe scaffolding instructional techniques and results from scaffolding. According to McKenzie (1999), scaffolding:

1. Provides clear directions and explain just what students must do in order to meet the expectations for the learning activity;
2. Clarifies purpose and keeps purpose and motivation in the forefront;
3. Keeps students on task so that the learner can exercise great personal discretion within parameters but is not in danger of off road stranding;
4. Offers assessment to clarify expectations right from the beginning as students are shown rubrics and standards that define excellence;
5. Points out students to worthy sources by allowing students to put their energy into interpretation rather than wandering;
6. Reduces uncertainty, surprise, and disappointment with a clear goal to maximize learning and efficiency;
7. Delivers efficiency, yet still requires hard work centered on the inquiry that it seems like a potter and wheel; and
8. Creates momentum as searching for understanding inspires and provokes (McKenzie, 1999).

In *Learning to Learn* Ngeow and Yoon (2001) explained a term called *problem-based learning* (PBL) which encourages children to develop learning practices. Scaffolded instruction is part of PBL. According to Ngeow and Yoon (2001) the More Knowledgeable Other ". . . designs activities which offer just enough of a scaffold for students to overcome this gap in knowledge and skills" (Ngeow & Yoon, 2001, p. 2).

As explained in *Thought and Language*, Vygotsky and Hanfmann (1967) pointed out that children develop an inner speech. This is a result of internalizing information after communicating with a More Knowledgeable Other. Vygotsky believed that inner speech, also called *private speech* leads to cognitive growth (Vygotsky & Hanfmann, 1967). Recent research studies confirm that scaffolding is a productive learning method. In *Visual Tools for Constructing Knowledge,* Hyerle (1996) uses various visual prompts as scaffolds to assist learners in remembering content. This method proved to be very beneficial for helping students to understand and remember content.

In addition to the literature, research studies show that scaffolding proves beneficial. Chang, Chen, and Sung (2002) conducted a seven week research study with 126 fifth graders to see if there would be a difference between scores when scaffolding was used versus when it was not used. Before the study began, the students were assigned to four random learning groups that included three levels of exposure to concept maps and one control group. Pre-tests and post-tests were given to test comprehension and summarization abilities. The four random learning groups were broken into map correction (most scaffolding), scaffold fading (moderate scaffolding), and map generation (least scaffolding). The test was administered at an elementary school in Taipei, Taiwan. There were sixty-six boys and sixty girls separated into groups containing 26, 32, 34, and 34 in the respective groups. The results of this study showed that the correction group (most scaffolding) scored higher on the post-test than the scaffold fading group, generation group, and the control group. The researchers point out that the map correction group excelled because of the scaffolding. Although the scaffold fading (moderate group) had some inconsistent scores, the researchers argued that they could be a result of content difficulty and lack of time for training (Chang, Chen, & Sung, 2002). In conclusion, this research study showed how concept mapping (scaffolding) ". . . may serve as a useful graphic strategy for improving text learning" (Chang, Chen, & Sung, 2002, p. 21).

Vygotsky's thinking ties greatly to a social and cultural background (Vygotsky & Cole, 1978). From a developmental perspective, Vygotsky believed that culture had a very important role on the development process. It is evident that the ideas of development and culture vary among researchers. Lamb (2005) stated that development is complex because culture is complicated to understand. Also, Lamb (2005) agrees that culture influences child behavior, social interaction, and more. School administrators and staff should take into consideration their school's culture and apply best practices for exposing students to learning opportunities on the school bus.

Discussion Questions for Chapter 3

1. What is the importance of a More Knowledgeable Other (MKO) on a school bus?
2. In what way can students benefit from a traveling school bus tutor on the school bus?
3. In your opinion, how many years will it take most American schools to transform school buses into "A Yellow Classroom?" Why?
4. What are the different ways children can learn while on the school bus?
5. In which ways is learning in the classroom similar to learning on the school bus?

Bus-stop 2 Bus-stop™ Journal Activity

Plan and sketch a school bus seating chart that encourages social learning. Imagine the bus has 20 3rd grade students (on grade level) and 20 6th grade students (on grade level). Write 5-6 sentences about your seating chart and explain any assigned bus seats.

CHAPTER 4

The Cafeteria: Academics
for Breakfast and Lunch

Why are students not learning
in the school cafeteria?

The school cafeteria is yet another overlooked area for learning. Dr. Gaines points out the importance of including academic content in the cafeteria. On average, students spend 10-15 minutes in the cafeteria for breakfast and 20-30 minutes in the cafeteria for lunch. This breakfast and lunch time can be multiplied by five school days a week. In most cases, students visit the school cafeteria at least once daily for lunch, whether he or she brings lunch or eats a school lunch. Since most school cafeterias allow student socialization, the cafeteria becomes useful as a social learning area.

In most elementary and middle schools in America, students are supervised in the cafeteria by their teachers. While students are eating, they can be exposed to academic content on educational placemats, television screens, posters, and other visual aids. Recent research shows that alternative learning areas (such as the school cafeteria) have explicit and direct connections to learning. They are a "safe way of creating flexibility to the shape of the school day, without requiring major change or disruption to teachers, pupils, staff, or parents" (Wood & Walker, 2007, p. 153).

The Breakfast Club: A Healthy Way to Learn

An example of a research study where students had increased learning time in the cafeteria was the Breakfast Club. This article is very informative and was published in The *Impact of Breakfast Clubs on Pupil Attendance and Punctuality* (Simpson, 2006). This study mixed breakfast time with structured and interesting learning activities. In this study, the breakfast club extended the school day to begin earlier than the normal time. The Breakfast Club was an effective avenue for promotion of nutrition and academic content during a usually informal and overlooked learning opportunity. The club provided at least one additional task to each breakfast. Also, the Breakfast Club provided additional learning as well as a healthy way to start the school day, which is extremely important for learning. The article gave three models on how this learning methodology worked. Each of these models were tested and proven to be effective (Simpson, 2006).

A Cafeteria Placemat Research Study by Dr. Gaines

For her dissertation study, Dr. Keshia L. Gaines conducted a research study using various educational placemats in a school cafeteria. Her dissertation title is "A Quantitative Study of Learning in the School Cafeteria Using Educational Placemats." In this research study Dr. Gaines studied the differences in student achievement before and after students were exposed to educational placemats in a school cafeteria. The students were exposed to the four different placemats for four days each. The student's gender and ability group was considered in relation to the pre-test and post-test scores. This study included 49 ability grouped third grade students in an elementary school in south Mississippi. Students were pre-tested with researcher-made tests before the educational placemats were introduced and post-tested afterwards. The following table shows descriptive information about the pre-tests, post-tests, and cafeteria placemats.

PRE-TESTS, POST-TESTS, AND PLACEMATS

Order	Color	Content	Corresponding Test
Placemat #1	Yellow	Fractions	Fractions Tests
Placemat #2	Pink	Solar System	Lines/Angles Test
Placemat #3	Teal	2D and 3D Shapes	Shapes Test
Placemat #4	Light Blue	Parts of Speech	Perimeter Test

For research purposes, some of the placemats served as a control factor and did not relate to the pre-test and post-test content. Dr. Gaines measured the differences in scores using a mixed model ANOVA in SPSS statistical software. Two of the hypotheses proposed a significant increase in learning (pre-test and post-test) by both gender and ability group.

The cafeteria placemats with math (same concepts on cafeteria placemats and tests) showed a significant academic improvement after cafeteria placemat exposure. In other words, students had higher testing averages after exposure to math educational placemats in the school cafeteria. In contrast the cafeteria placemats without math showed a decrease in test averages after cafeteria placemat exposure. While students who were exposed to mathematical content on their placemats scored significantly higher on their post-tests.

Music and Audio in the School Cafeteria

Many formal and fast-food restaurants use music and/or audio advertising to persuade customers. In this same fashion, schools can use music or audio in the school cafeteria to change the student's moods and teach academic content. It is very important that the school cafeteria creates a welcoming atmosphere for relaxation and social learning.

Chapter 4 Research Focus:
Visual Learning with Visual Learning Tools

Scientific research goes to support a higher degree of effectiveness when visual learning is involved. It is usually more effective than other learning methods such as kinesthetic learning or auditory learning. As stated in Jensen, "Between 80 and 90 percent of all information that is absorbed by our brains is visual" (Jensen, 2008, p. 55). Mayer and Sims (1994) conducted a study on the use of visual learning strategies. These were conducted within four key areas.

The first is a survey of learning theories which use visual and graphic organizers. The second key area is the benefits of using visual learning strategies in the development of literacy. This study also considers how visual organizers (such as charts, graphs, etc.) are used in the development of learning and thinking skills. This study also takes into consideration other issues such as retention, problem solving, critical thinking and note taking. Finally, another consideration is the use of visual organizers for other kinds of classroom activities.

In Paivio (1991), more than two-thirds of students at all levels have benefited from the use of non-traditional visual learning in mastering their vocabulary skills. It was also found that students who focused more on visual learning strategies improved their writing skills at a faster rate compared to those who used other methods. Pavio (1986) believes visual aids fall under three categories. The three categories are: task-specific organizers, thinking process maps, and brainstorming webs. Under each of these categories lie graphic, or visual, organizers which are unique. For the task-specific organizers there are life cycles as applied in science, decision trees as applied in mathematics, and text structures as applied in reading. Paivio (1986) considers graphic organizers as being comprised of all of the above. Throughout this study the term graphic organizers is used interchangeably with the term visual organizers.

Researchers, Jowett and Linton (1989) discovered that students who used graphic organizers significantly improved in their cognitive as well as their critical thinking skills when compared to those who used different or alternative learning methods. Further, Danan (1992), and Kleinman and Dwyer (1999) found that students' retention and recall abilities were improved with the use of these visual learning strategies. This was true even with the students with learning disabilities. When follow-ups were done at various intervals, it was found that those who learned through visual methods retained and recalled more information. The use of graphic organizers was found to improve students' ability to transfer, recall, and retain skills and apply them to situations completely new to them (Mayer, 2001). Benson (1997) conducted a study of eight senior high school students. He found that visual learning was a very helpful aid for these students to develop essential skills. These students had disabilities in learning social studies, but were able to improve with visual aids.

Graphic organizers are of great importance because they aid in the processing and storage of information. Paivio (1986) observed that visual organizers had the effect of enhancing "nonlinguistic representation development" (aka visual tools) in students and therefore strengthened their development in academic content.

According to Horn (1998), the use of visual learning enables students to increase knowledge, but this could benefit from the combination of visual basics and words. Horn (1998) reports that over the past 50 years additional words have been added to medical, diagramming, and engineering illustrations.

The dual coding theory developed by Paivio (1986) is one that has attracted great interest from many educators due to its various implications in education. This theory supports utilization of visual aids which lead to positively enhanced learning. Danan (1992) adds to this debate in his argument that teachers who use various visual learning aids stand a greater chance of improving their students' interaction and motivation in both academic and non-academic activities. Visual aids are also considered helpful to the teachers because they offer practical solutions to many problems encountered in the teaching process.

Campbell and Stanley (1993) conducted a study on the significance of application of visual learning in the study of mathematics. In order to facilitate the study, students were required to participate using both virtual and physical manipulatives (hands on objects). The first group was required to participate in lessons on fractions using physical manipulatives, while the second group was to participate in lessons using virtual manipulatives. Phase two required them to do the opposite. The entire test was made up of three sections. The first section included items that were dual coded and presented through both number and picture representation. Part two consisted of items that had only numeric representation. The third part had word problems that required drawing pictures and explaining the possible solutions. As a result, students who used pictures performed much better than those without pictures.

Pictures have been found to have excellent effectiveness in terms of producing desired results. When teaching young children, pictures play an important role in helping children associate pictures with new words. Not every word can have a pictorial representation. This is because some words are rather abstract and lack real representation in the world (Anderson and Shifrin, 1980). Nevertheless, visual memory is considered to be retained more than any other kind of learning in human beings. Anderson and Shifrin (1980) argue that this is the very reason why dictionaries are often inclusive of pictures in the explanation of words.

Mayer & Sims (1994) and Gallick-Jackson (1997), conducted research in an attempt to determine what effect visual organizers had on writing skills. Their studies involved 2nd and 3rd grade students with two teachers who were conducting their master's projects. The intention was to establish whether the student's creative, narrative, and composition writing skills could be improved. For that matter, the experiments integrated graphic organizers, word processing, and art in the process of writing. The classes were divided into two, so that one group was instructed using graphic organizers, and the other without. These experiments went on over a 12 week period, and the pre and post-tests results show that the students with graphic organizers excelled more in their creative, narrative and composition writing skills than those students who were instructed without them. It was further established that once students were introduced to visual organizers, they preferred them over other instructional aids.

The use of photographic, or eidetic, memory has been seriously contested, and not as many studies have been conducted to certify its existence. According to Kleinman and Dwyer (1999), there is strong evidence that photographic memory exists, but there is still very little understanding of this concept. Recent literature explains that even where it exists, it is found in less than ten percent of the entire human population. Horn (1998) states that photographic memory is quite often found in children, but is easily lost before adulthood. Its rarity is the main reason why many do not find credibility in the claims of its existence. Horn (1998) and Silverman (2002) debate whether possessing this kind of memory is positive or negative, especially since too much information can overwhelm a person and may reduce the ability to recall. As far as visual learning is concerned, the use of cafeteria placemats or other visual (and auditory) learning opportunities will increase academic exposure in the cafeteria.

Tools to Implement Learning in the Cafeteria

1. Use educational placemats on the cafeteria tables
2. Use TV screens with educational programming
3. Use audio (music) to alter mood, behavior, or to educate
4. Use small posters on the cafeteria tables
5. Use educational content on the interior walls of the cafeteria

Discussion Questions for Chapter 4

1. What are two learning tools that can help students learn academic content in the school cafeteria?
2. In your opinion, do you think teacher supervision will affect the successfulness of learning in the cafeteria?
3. How will the five tools change learning in the school cafeteria?
4. In which ways is learning in the school cafeteria similar to learning on the school bus?
5. What other methods can you create to enhance students learning in the school cafeteria?

Bus-stop 2 Bus-stop™ Journal Activity

Observe one formal restaurant and one fast-food restaurant. Write 5 ways that school cafeterias are alike and different from public restaurants.

CHAPTER 5

The Bathroom: An Independent Study and Other Controversial Areas to Learn

Why are students not learning in other non-traditional areas?

Traditionally, students have used the school's bathroom for more than toiletry needs. Fights, bullying, cursing, and even drug use occurs in many school bathrooms of the twenty-first century. Negative actions of all sorts have reportedly taken place in elementary, middle, and high school bathroom stalls across America. Students realize that the inside of the bathroom has very little, if any, supervision by teachers and staff. School leaders and others can prevent a school's bathroom area from becoming a haven for bullying, skipping class, or drug and tobacco use.

Unlike other Bus-stop 2 Bus-stop™ methods, a school's bathroom can serve as a brief and independent study session. Instead of using school bathrooms for toiletry needs only, an educational component should be present. This educational component can take form as academic posters, television screens, and/or audio systems. Adding educational components to the interior of a school's bathroom could serve two purposes:

1. Purpose #1—Adding educational content to the school's bathroom will increase academic achievement. Research has shown in current literature the effects of incidental learning on students. (see research section on incidental learning)
2. Purpose #2—Adding educational content to the school's bathroom may decrease the amount of fights, bullying, cursing, and even drug use. Research has shown that students are less likely to get into trouble if they are in a structured environment with purpose.

School bathrooms consist of separate areas for boys and girls. With this in mind, a school administrator can plan gender-specific academic designs for each bathroom's interior. Learning styles and preferences differ amongst boys and girls. In some cases, mathematic achievement is related to a student's gender and interest in mathematics. Using current data, a school can pinpoint their academic areas of concern according to a gender breakdown.

Gender roles are very important in today's society. When children are young, parents buy toys, clothes, and other items according to a child's gender. Stereotypical careers are mentioned for boys such as a doctor, lawyer, engineer, or even President of the United States. In contrast, parents may mention careers for girls, but many of them still assume that one day they will grow into the role of a wife and mother.

Society has certain expectations for boys that differ from the expectations for girls. These expectations generate varying patterns of behavior and reactions according to the child's gender. Gender roles should be considered when designing a gender-specific bathroom area for students.

The choir room, football stadium, gym, tennis court, and swimming pool areas can use the Bus-stop 2 Bus-stop™ method to increase student exposure to academic content. In consideration of the school's goal for academic achievement outside the classroom, extra-curricular activities should use the Bus-stop 2 Bus-stop™ method as well. The classroom is an obvious place that academic content should be displayed. Before using the Bus-stop 2 Bus-stop™ method, a school's administration and staff should examine the school and community's culture. Schools that embrace student learning are more likely to be successful with the Bus-stop 2 Bus-stop™ learning method.

In order to enhance student learning, schools must encourage students to learn in areas outside the classroom. Purposefully educational activities in non-traditional areas such as the school gym, choir room, and video arcade rooms will provide a valued learning experience for the student. According to past research, out-of-classroom exposure to educational material is beneficial because it exposes students to the following things:

1. Complex thinking skills
2. Social skills with peers
3. Application of knowledge
4. Building self-confidence and individuality
5. Decision making
6. Social learning opportunities

How can schools implement this?

First and foremost, schools should analyze their school environment. Starting at the bus stop, school stakeholders should examine all school areas to find new areas for teaching and learning. After these non-traditional areas are identified, a plan should be put into place to change these areas into learning opportunities.

The Educational Video Arcade

A video arcade room can be a fun, alternative learning area. In addition to the educational component, some games can mix exercise with educational content and engaging games. Usually, video arcade games are in public businesses such as movie theatres, restaurants, amusement parks, local fairs, etc. Most games are categorized as pinball games, electronic video games, games to win merchandise, or sports/recreation games.

Coin-operated machines provide an engaging atmosphere for youth and teens. The 1920's amusement park inspired today's arcade games. As early as the 1930's, coin-operated pinball machines were used. Why can't schools offer educational games as an alternative learning opportunity or as an incentive for good behavior?

Children enjoy games that involve points, animations, racing games, vehicle combat games which are equipped with joysticks and buttons, and repetitive memory games.

Music Recording Studio

Some students enjoy writing and recording music. Since music and rhythm helps students learn academic content, students should have an area to create and record music on the school campus. The music teacher can create lessons that integrate math, language, and other curriculums with music. The recording sessions may be awarded as an incentive or as a part of a mandatory class assignment.

Automated Teacher Robots

As an alternative, some students could rely on automated teachers whom ask and answer questions about academic content. These automated teacher robots can assist students during educational down-times and transition areas. Giving students a choice is one of the most important lesson design qualities. Some students may prefer to work individually with computerized lessons from an automated teacher robot. This unique learning robot for the future will provide students with an alternative method for learning.

Amusement Park-Type School:
The Schools of the Future

Imagine a non-stop fun learning experience in American schools. Color, music, and hands on activities could be mixed with academic content. At a glance, the school would look similar to a local carnival or fun park. At second glance, a bystander would realize that all games, activities, etc. are related to district, state, and national academic standards. Any inside-the-classroom instruction will take place solely to help students with writing, formal lessons, and test taking.

Chapter 5 Research Focus:
Characteristics of a Successful School

A successful school has many characteristics. A successful school has an environment conducive to learning, staff member collaboration, new teacher support systems, and effective leadership and supervision. The first characteristic of a successful school is that it has a pleasant work environment for teachers and a great learning environment for students.

> "When we grasp the underlying values of our particular school as a work environment, we can consciously act to reshape the organization into a purposeful collection of individuals who believe that schools are for students, for learning, and for improvement rather than for insularity, self-protection, and complacency." (Glickman Gordon, & Ross-Gordon, pg. 20)

Collaboration amongst teachers will ensure success because professional isolation can lead to psychological isolation. Successful schools also have good new teacher induction programs and new teacher support systems. The retention of quality teachers is critical to a schools stability, growth, and success. Effective leadership and supervision of these new teachers and veteran teachers play an important role in the outcome of the Bus-stop 2 Bus-stop™ learning method.

> "Leaders recognized that the student's day does not really begin in the classroom, but on the bus or perhaps during free breakfast. By committing their systems to consistency in the education and behavior of adults, these leaders ensure that every adult leader, from the bus driver to the food service employee to the classroom teacher is regarded as a significant adult leader in the eyes of students"(Reeves, 2004, pg.199).

Also, successful schools have school-wide involvement in curriculum and instructional decisions. "If teachers don't see each other at work, don't talk with each other about their work, and see teaching as what goes on within their own four walls, it is not surprising that they are not given the opportunity, time, or expectations to be involved in decisions about curriculum and instruction beyond their four walls." (Glickman, 2010, pg. 29)

What about Bus-stop 2 Bus-stop™ in high risk schools?

According to Douglas Reeves, a 90-90-90 school is a successful school which is made of low economic students and minority students. In Reeves (2004), the *90-90-90 Schools* research article claimed that low-income schools with a 90% or above minority population could be successful with appropriate instructional practices and strategies. Several key factors such as consistency, writing strategies, and collaboration of teacher ideas and assessments made these specific schools productive. This study also argued that "the key variable was not poverty, but teaching quality" (Reeves, 2004, pg. 194). He stated that there is a positive correlation between great classroom strategies, performance assessments, and student achievement.

Similar to the Bus-stop 2 Bus-stop™ method, *90-90-90 Schools* use collaboration and cross-disciplinary integration techniques, which both involve social learning. Other characteristics of a 90-90-90 school are that above 90% of students receive free or reduced lunch, above 90% of students are from ethnic minorities, and above 90% achieved high academic standards. In alignment with the high academic standards, these schools display exemplary work throughout the school. "In short, the 90/90/90 Schools made it clear to even the most casual observer that academic performance was highly prized" (Reeves, 2004, pg. 187). The culture of the school played a very important part in the student's achievement.

An accountability system was in place during Reeves (2004) study that mandated schools to identify areas where improvements were made. Since many of the students entered school being severely below grade level, the schools targeted a few goal areas instead of a typical school plan that often includes many unfocused goals. In many cases a type of literary intervention was implemented, since deficiencies in writing and reading severely hinder all subject areas. Weekly assessments were conducted by classroom teachers to monitor student progress and multiple opportunities were provided to improve performance. Written response assessments allowed the teachers to obtain specific information about the individual student's ability, and the students were also able to demonstrate their thinking processes. The papers were then exchanged and graded on a uniform basis by several teachers and sometimes the principal of the school. Once the assessments were evaluated, the students were provided with teacher's feedback. This immediate feedback to students included precise details on student strengths and weaknesses to guide the students' progress. In return, the teacher's high expectations were eventually met by the students (Reeves, 2004).

The time schedules of most 90-90-90 Schools were altered to increase academic learning time in subjects at the elementary and secondary levels. School accountability plans and other action plans were flexible so that non-effective strategies could be changed as needed. Principals often reassigned teachers to different grade levels or subject areas according to their undergraduate areas of study and expertise. Also, other employees such as bus drivers, cafeteria workers, and janitorial staff were included in professional development opportunities to ensure the school could be consistent with its overall goals.

Music, art, physical education, and other elective classes were also held accountable for additional academic achievement. The plan for success in these schools was collaboration between all school employees and any others that could impact the student's education. Ultimately, for a 90-90-90 School to be successful, it had to have effective teachers and leadership teams that are willing to be accountable for student performance (Reeves, 2004).

Discussion Questions for Chapter 5

1. In your opinion, what is the best method for students to learn academic content in the school bathroom? Video, audio, or posters as visual aids?
2. In your opinion, which age group and gender will receive the greatest benefit from learning in the bathroom? Boys or girls? High school, middle school, or elementary students?
3. What two purposes could be served by adding a video arcade room to an elementary school?
4. What makes (or does not make) the school bathroom a controversial area for students to learn? Why?
5. In which ways is learning in the bathroom alike and different from learning in the school cafeteria?

Bus-stop 2 Bus-stop™ Journal Activity

Using a computer design program, create one boy's bathroom and one girl's bathroom with math and language themed content. Use gender-specific colors, themes, and items for student interest. Write two to three sentences that explain your designs.

CHAPTER 6

The Playground: A Fun Place to Learn

Why are students not learning on the playground?

The playground should be targeted as a primary area for students to learn academic content. Since most students enjoy visiting and playing on the playground, their interest level is very high. The playground can become an area for brain-based learning because it mixes physical movement, academic content, and high student interest. This mixture relates to brain-based learning and brain-based education, which are methods the brain learns best.

As defined by Jensen (2008), "Brain-based education is the engagement of strategies based on principals derived from an understanding of the brain" (p. 4). Since the brain serves to control and coordinate mental and physical actions in the body, it is very important to understand how the brain naturally learns best (Jensen, 2008).

Recently, educators have become interested in the brain and how it affects learning. Many schools and organizations have incorporated brain-based research and brain-based learning strategies into their daily routines. Researchers have continued to produce literature geared completely towards brain-based learning. Many educators have abandoned traditional instructional techniques and have adopted brain-based strategies. These strategies include learner participation and engaging lessons, which can be easily taught on the playground. A quote from an English Language Learner (ELL) teacher in Lombardi (2008) provided an innovative way to approach brain-compatible learning.

> "Teaching around the wheel—using the full range of auditory, visual, and kinesthetic strategies-activity shifting, instructional intelligence, multiple intelligences, and an array of diverse teaching approaches all tap in to the best of brain-compatible learning and provide innovative ways to reach students" (Lombardi, 2008, p. 219).

Despite the new and informative research on brain-based learning, the area is still being explored. Alferink and

Farmer-Dougan (2010) pointed out how difficult it is to understand how brain-based research can lead to misinterpretation of the information. The authors continue to explain how brain-based research is over-interpreted when weak evidence presents itself. Overall, brain-based research studies have attempted to fill in the gap of literature on this topic.

In *Teaching and the Human Brain*, Caine and Caine (1994) highlighted the importance of the left and right hemispheres of the brain when conducting activities. They go on to explain the past myth of associating the left and right hemispheres with certain brain functions. Throughout history, the two parts were thought to control specific tasks only. Caine and Caine (1994) argue that the right hemisphere processes information in whole, while the left hemisphere only processes information in parts. In their book, they support findings about how the parts of the brain interact within itself. Also, they agree that the two hemispheres support each other. They believe that progress can be made when effective brain-based strategies are used while being mindful of both hemispheres of the brain.

In an article titled *A Fresh Look at Brain-Based Education*, Jensen (2008) opposed researcher Bruer's (1997a) beliefs of neuroscience being useless for educators. Bruer was a researcher for the James S. McDonnell Foundation. He stated that educators should focus on learning psychology instead of neuroscience. Jensen (2008) disagreed with Bruer because he thinks that brain-based learning can improve education by allowing teachers to make decisions that will greatly increase student academic achievement.

Similar to playing on the playground, brain development occurs during certain periods of a person's lifetime. Studies report that certain brain development begins as early as two months of age. Research shows that babies begin observing their surroundings during this time. In Lindsey (1998-1999), a series of experiments were reviewed from the 1960's and 1970's to explore the learning windows for children. In these experiments, two researchers examined the brain development of sight in multiple kittens. The study concluded that the brains of the kittens developed sight during a certain time frame, similar to humans. Jorgenson (2003) argued against this research, and states that this research has been enhanced with fictitious content. He states, "These windows of opportunity have been embellished far beyond original research findings" (Jorgenson, 2003, p. 364). When considering learning on the playground, brain-based research must be adequately tested before all of its capabilities will be understood. Educators can search for new brain-based research in order to create an environment conducive to brain-based learning.

There is a definitive gap in literature as to the effectiveness of brain-based teaching and learning practices, especially as it relates to learning on the playground. Current literature shows information on brain-based teaching practices, but there are not many studies done that test its overall effectiveness. Opinions and ideas are presented by many authors of research journals and textbooks, but few focus on learning on the playground. Research studies with formal statistical analysis would be a great help to fill the gap in educational literature.

In *Brain-Based Learning: A Synthesis of Research,* the National American Colleges and Teachers of Agriculture point out the need for agricultural teachers to use brain-based learning. It was expressed that students would learn better if the academic content had meaning and more real-word applications. Brain-based learning, when learning on the playground, is about memorization and making learning meaningful. In a journal article by Bucko (1997), it states the brain has a hundred billion neurons, and therefore is very capable of storing large amounts of information. He shared, "Brain-based learning may be the most important influence on the way we teach since the first school was founded" (Bucko, 1997, p. 20). He continues on to address implications for teachers and schools. One of Bucko's points involved the importance of technology in examining the brain's functions. He points out that neural imaging can also tell us pertinent information. Bucko (1997) promotes the use of brain-friendly techniques such as using meaning, repetition, patterning, and emotion. These brain-friendly techniques can be easily applied to learning on the playground.

Although there is a gap in literature on brain-based research testing with education, many researchers continue to support the brain-based movement. One can assume that authors such as Jensen and Dabney (2000) and Sousa (2003) make a significant amount of money from book sales, conferences, and other items or services sold to educational facilities on brain-based learning. It is in their best interest to point out the positive aspects of this research because it affects their monetary gain and career status. Some researchers argue against this misapplication of brain-based research, yet still continue to provide reasonable uses for it to advance education.

Over-analyzing Playground Play

In *Brain-(not) Based Education: Dangers of Misunderstanding and Misapplication of Neuroscience*, Alferink and Farmer-Dougan (2010) claimed that incorporating neuroscience into teaching strategies "goes beyond existing data" and is "not supported by current evidence." The article continued on to critique four alleged neuroscience-based practices as follows:

1. "Right" vs. "Left" Brain Instruction,
2. The Brain and Critical Periods,
3. Brain-based Education, and
4. Brain-compatible teaching, Learning Styles, and Multiple Intelligences (Alferink and Farmer-Dougan, 2010, p. 43-48)

In summary, this article claimed that brain-based research is helpful for educators to realize best educational practices, but it should be used correctly (Alferink & Farmer-Dougan, 2010). In other words, teachers and educators can use brain-based strategies in planning their lessons, but must be aware that brain-based research is very complicated. For the sake of applying academic content to the playground area, only a limited knowledge of brain-based research is necessary.

Gatewood (1989) also criticized the popularity of brain-based learning. He questioned the acceptance of brain research and its application to education. In his opinion, researchers do not know enough about the brain, therefore further studies should be conducted. In his article *Caution!*

Applying Brain Research to Education, (1989) he argued that completely restructuring schools on account of this little amount of research is not advisable. Although he does not support implementing brain-based learning, he does not provide a data-driven reason for the lack of support.

According to Jones (1995), a gap exists between brain research and education. He points out how strategies within brain research and education contradict each other. For example, education encourages stress-free environments while brain-based learning encourages stress (helpful stress called eustress) to help students remember. Another example is that education encourages explanations instead of memorizations, while brain-research encourages meaningful memorization and repetition (Jones, 1995). He also briefly highlighted three areas of concern from scientists which are early learning, abstract reasoning with music, and healthy diet.

Learning on the Playground: An Early Window of Learning Opportunity

Greenspan (2000) explained how a human's window of learning opportunity will not occur again once it has passed. This window occurs in a person's early years of life. Educational salespersons take advantage of this knowledge and use it in various advertisements. Bergen (2002) shared, "Catalogs for educational products now tout the links between the products and specific areas of brain development, and parents are urged to buy many products purporting to stimulate development of certain skills during early 'critical periods' for children's brains" (p. 376). Although this tactic is common, brain-based techniques prove very beneficial to youth and adolescents (Bergen, 2002).

Assessing a student's learning style first is an idea of Dunn and Griggs (2000). Their book, *Practical Approaches to Using Learning Styles in Higher Education* explains about the many unique learning styles of learners. They strongly support the idea of getting to know a student's learning style before beginning instruction. After the learning style has been identified, the educator can then apply the appropriate teaching techniques and methods to help the student. This consideration has been known to make the students comfortable in the learning environment (Dunn & Griggs, 2000).

Morgan (1999) echoes other researchers about the developing study of brain-based trends. He points out that many educators have a desire to learn brain-based teaching techniques. An article in Psychology Today agrees that "Teachers try to change the brain every day. The more they know about how it learns, the more successful they can be" (Chance, 2001, p. 72).

According to Chance (2001), brain-based researchers have found the following things true about neuroscience as it relates to education:

1. An environment conducive to brain-based learning will help students. Educators should provide games, tasks, and activities to challenge the brain;
2. The proper amount of sleep helps brain functions. It is a good idea to encourage students to get an adequate amount of sleep; and

3. Stress (bad stress) can affect the brain and destroy brain cells. Educators should provide a less stressful learning environment (Chance, 2001, p. 72).

What will teachers think about Teaching on the Playground?

According to Bruer (1997b) teachers that support brain-based education, such as teaching on the playground, are generally open-minded. He states that brain-based educators do not practice old-fashioned teaching methods where the teachers present information for students to learn only to meet compliance. In fact, these teachers incorporate physical activities into the general instruction. It is important to note that students on the playground can learn independently or with teacher assistance. In chapter six of Eric Jensen's book, "The Impact of Physical Movement on the Brain," Jensen (2008) detailed the importance of physical movement on the brain.

> Exercise does several things for the brain. First, it enhances circulation so that individual neurons can get more oxygen and nutrients. This means a great deal when you're teaching content and you need the brain to be at its best. Second, it may spur the production of nerve growth factor, a hormone that enhances brain function. Third, gross motor repetitive movements can stimulate the production of dopamine, a mood-enhancing neurotransmitter.

Finally, when done in sufficient amounts, we know that exercise enhances the production of new cells in the brain. (Jensen, 2008, p. 38)

Educational Games on the Playground

Likewise, Jensen (2008) shared the benefits of engaging students by using social activities such as games. According to Jensen (2008), educators should be mindful of curriculum that considers the brain. In Figure 21.2 on page 203, Jensen (2008) showed the five things to consider when designing curriculum with the brain in mind: information literacy, scientific inquiry, artistic expression, social fluency, and personal development (Jensen, 2008). Other educators agree that "games can provide an active, motivating way for students to review what they've learned, but their effectiveness is enhanced if the students participate in the design or construction of the game" (Wolfe, 2001, p. 187). In the opinion of brain-based theorists, activities help young learners, in particular, because they include movement. Blakemore (2003) agrees and states that "Writing or talking about an idea often provides enough muscle movement, but some people think best while they are swimming, running, or shaving, all of which involve movement" (p. 22). Jensen and Dabney (2000) also agree that movement and physical exercise help to stimulate the brain.

In an article by Prigge (2002), she suggested using laughter in the classroom as a brain-based approach. Prigge claimed that the body reacts biochemically to humor. Also, humor helps to reduce stress (bad stress) and create a better atmosphere. In addition to humor, Prigge recommended allowing movement and activities for oxygen flow to the brain. Prigge also recommended engaging activities with manipulatives, which can be easily introduced on the playground.

In *Understanding a Brain-based Approach to Learning and Teaching*, Caine and Caine (1990) argued that the most complicated part of brain-based learning is understanding the capabilities of the human brain. As pointed out in this article, "this information requires a major shift in our definitions of testing and grading and in the organizational structure of schools" (Caine & Caine, 1990, pg. 66). This article pinpointed the following principles for learning that can work as a theoretical foundation of brain-based learning:

1. The brain is a parallel processor
2. Learning Engages the Entire Physiology
3. The search for meaning is innate
4. The search for meaning occurs through 'patterning'
5. Emotions are critical to patterning
6. Every brain simultaneously perceives and creates parts and wholes
7. Learning involves both focused attention and peripheral perception
8. Learning always involves conscious and unconscious processes
9. We have two types of memory: A spatial memory system and a set of systems for rote learning
10. The brain understands and remembers best when facts and skills are embedded in natural spatial memory
11. Learning is enhanced by challenge and inhibited by threat
12. Each brain is unique (Caine & Caine, 1990, pg. 66-69).

Brain-based educators largely support a constructive model for students to become actively engaged in learning (Bruer, 1997b). In *Perspectives on Learning*, Vygotsky's theory of social learning is mentioned as a highly compatible brain-based theory (Phillips & Soltis, 1998). In Bruer, (1997a), he accuses brain-based learning of not being beneficial to teachers, but he adds that it is very fascinating. In addition to Bruer (1997a), Blakemore (2003) realizes that brain-based education still needs to expand in research. "Human understanding of the brain is in its infancy, and much research needs to be done" (Blakemore, 2003, p. 22).

Also, Davis (2000) realizes that brain-based research does not have many studies done in this area. Bruer (1997b) echoes this belief that neuroscientists have just begun exploring this field of study.

Special Education Students Can Learn on the Playground Too

Since brain-based learning includes special education students, Levine and Barringer (2008) point out the emotional perspective of some students with learning disabilities. "A student's inability to keep pace with the demands of the classroom can produce feelings of inadequacy, performance anxiety, depleted motivation, and even behavioral maladjustment" (Levine and Barringer, 2008, pg. 9). With special education students, brain-based learning is beneficial because it takes into account the student's emotions and brain differences. In this journal article, difficulties with learning are pointed out to be brain-based dysfunctions (Levine & Barringer, 2008). Since the students in this article have learning difficulties, their teacher can benefit from using brain-based practices. In alignment with brain-based education's consideration of emotions, the article advises teachers to use a positive approach while helping children. "In helping children who are delayed in learning, its especially important to diagnose and manage their strengths, because positive findings sometimes can be used to help bypass obstructive dysfunctions" (Levine & Barringer, 2008, pg. 11).

In Jensen's book (1996), *Completing the Puzzle: The Brain-based Approach,* he encourages giving the students choices when giving them assignments. This supposedly benefits the brain by reducing stress and therefore increasing endorphin release. Without these choices, the brain may not release endorphins and may lead to decreased learning. Jensen (1996) recommends creating areas, similar to the educational playground areas, which are intellectually stimulating and comfortable for students. To meet the physical needs of the brain (especially on the playground), students should be well nourished and hydrated (Hruby, 1999).

Sidewalks Near the Playground and School: Walk and Learn

As students are walking from class to the playground, they observe their surroundings on the sidewalk and nearby areas. Many schools post student work samples, art projects, or other student work in out-of-classroom areas, but do not include academic learning content there. If academic content was added to the school's sidewalks and playground areas it would increase academic achievement of students. Sidewalks often surround playgrounds, basketball courts, and other outside areas. Repetition, visual learning, and especially incidental learning play a part while students are exposed to academic content in these playground areas.

Chapter 6 Research Focus: Incidental Learning on the Playground

Incidental learning refers to the unintentional learning that results from informal learning activities. As a learning process, incidental learning takes place through repetition, observation, social interaction activities, and problem solving situations. Learning under these conditions is considered to be made of assumptions, beliefs and values, hidden agenda, trial and error, and involvement which can be inferred from events (Bender & Larkin, 2009). Incidental learning may occur when a student unconsciously glances at the sidewalk or playground equipment while playing on the playground. It is evident that educators are able to analyze how learning from visual aids on physical education equipment or on a sidewalk can affect students. Incidental learning can help the students in terms of improved competence, attitude change, and growth in interpersonal skills, raised self-awareness, and many other desirable impacts on learning (O'Neil & Marsick, 2007).

The study of incidental learning is well established. Researcher E.J. Brophy (2010) states that primary producers of research on incidental learning are mainly from psychologists and educators. Most of these studies have concentrated on learning from observation and social interactions; some studies contend that the recall of incidental information among elementary students is greater with the usage of pictures than words. This is important to remember when creating incidental learning opportunities for areas where students play and interact. When considering informal and incidental learning among elementary students, it is important to note that Marsick and Watkins (1990) state that these learning types seem to be interconnected. Marsick and Watkins (1990) define incidental learning as a by-product of another activity such as trial and error experimentation.

In order to understand how incidental learning affects elementary students, it is important to note that incidental learning is unplanned. In most cases of incidental learning, a student will have a learning experience without any previous intention. Even though it is unintentional, incidental learning affects the unconscious learning of a person by visual memory.

Another area where incidental learning affects the students at the elementary level is language or vocabulary learning development. This is because through observation and social interaction the students develop a visual association with the carefully designed hallways, sidewalks, and floors. At one point, they are able to associate the pictures and words written on the sidewalks and playground equipment with their existing knowledge on the subject. Furthermore, considering that incidental learning may occur outside classroom at any Bus-stop 2 Bus-stop™ area, it may also tie into social learning. Playgrounds and sidewalks provide a favorable learning environment because social interaction takes place there. This environment presents an opportunity for students to build relationships among other students from the classroom (O'Neil & Marsick, 2007). In contrast to non-traditional or incidental learning, Boucher and Wiseman (2011) assert that meanings of words can be acquired through normal reading of texts, with no emphasis on vocabulary or visual learning outside the classroom.

A series of studies have confirmed that incidental learning can help children in multiple positive ways. Some of the effective ways in which incidental learning can help students is though improving their basic recall, especially in vocabulary, pictures, and mathematical concepts. In addition to basic recall, research has verified that children in elementary schools are able to learn the words' meaning incidentally from the context during reading and this forms the main source of vocabulary growth (Boucher & Wiseman, 2011; Jonson, Cappelloni & Niesyn, 2011). Considering that the playground area for elementary students is supervised by their teacher, who monitors student behavior, there may be greater opportunities for them to undergo incidental learning through oral language (Brophy, 2010). The existing empirical evidence indicates that young children who are encouraged to hear and experiment with language are more likely to achieve early reading success. Children who have limited experiences with language often have trouble learning to read and remain at risk for learning difficulties (Greenwood, 2010).

Another impact of informal and incidental learning is on the growth of interpersonal skills. Through social interaction, students are likely to develop social awareness, self-awareness, and certain social skills such as good listening habits, heightened observational styles, and greater general interaction with other students (Boucher & Wiseman, 2011). Incidental learning in the form of observing a visual aid placed on the playground will most likely change the student's behavior and social interaction with other students. Some authors acknowledge that unintended learning occurs outside the educational context and provides a motivational and enjoyable opportunity for students to interact with each other, therefore impacting their interpersonal skills (Brophy, 2010).

Incidental learning from observation and social interaction can help the students to acquire problem solving skills in addition to formal training (Marsick & Watkins, 1990). As it is noted, incidental learning appears to be a socialization process. This makes it easy for educators to create incidental learning outcomes. Teachers can encourage their students to develop critical reflection skills and facilitate activities in non-traditional learning areas of the school. These areas may be socially interactive areas that embed informal learning and incidental learning experiences (Greenwood, 2010).

Incidental learning can also help in the intellectual development of many students. A significant amount of learning occurs informally and incidentally beyond standard teaching in the classroom. Many students will attempt to apply some of the learned experiences in their small-group interactions, peer stories, and even in classroom discussions as they proceed with their education (Brophy, 2010).

With incidental learning, students encompass a wide range of activities where they can acquire knowledge through informally interacting with the environment around them. Boucher and Wiseman (2011) agree that incidental learning has some shortcomings (including the inability to measure the knowledge attained through it), due to its informal nature. Many students may also lack the ability to completely self-direct their learning. In conclusion, students can use the playground environment to make observations, complete tasks, and interact with others, and unknowingly acquire knowledge.

Discussion Questions for Chapter 6

1. How do you think America's public and private schools will benefit from academic content on the school's playgrounds and sidewalks?
2. In your opinion, what subject areas would students learn best while on the playground?
3. How could schools ensure that students are exposed to learning on the playground?
4. What are three main ways for students to be exposed to academic content on the playground using the Bus-stop 2 Bus-stop™ method?
5. In what ways are learning on the playground alike and different from the other Bus-stop 2 Bus-stop™ learning areas?

Bus-stop 2 Bus-stop™ Journal Activity

Write a lesson plan that is taught primarily on a school playground. Include hands on activities, writing assignments, etc. for students to complete on the school's playground. Include educational games for students to play on a nearby sidewalk. Include the use of sidewalk chalk.

CHAPTER 7

Bus-stop 2 Bus-stop™ Educational Clothing for Faculty, Staff, and Students

Why are students not learning from educational clothing?

New back-to-school fashions are looking exciting! Inner-city students are wearing clothing that has a purpose. This clothing is educational!

Students in various schools, including some in New York City, Los Angeles, and Miami, are catching on to the new fashion trend which pairs educational content, clothing, and catchy designs. The students like the clothing because it is trendy and includes bright colors.

"Wearing clothes with stuff from school is the new thing now," said a fifth grade student in Long Island, NY.

The clothing was designed by Dr. Keshia L. Gaines, creator of Bus-stop 2 Bus-stop™ educational products and services. Dr. Gaines envisioned an innovative way for students to learn academic content during the school day. Her book explains how students can learn at the bus stop, on the school bus, in the cafeteria, on the playgrounds, and more.

"Why are students not learning on the school bus?" Dr. Gaines asks superintendents and school officials across America. "Students can learn from non-traditional methods such as academic clothing or shoes. Why aren't we using these methods to teach the students?"

Bus-stop 2 Bus-stop™ clothing is available for purchase online. The company has hats, shirts, jackets, tote bags, and other custom-made products. This unique fashion trend has caught national attention of retail buyers, celebrities, and media. According to youth and teens, the most popular Bus-stop 2 Bus-stop™ clothing item is the educational t-shirts which include multiplication facts in various designs and colors.

Despite the slow U.S. economic recovery, youth and teens are constantly buying clothes. Dr. Gaines plans to introduce the newest Bus-stop 2 Bus-stop™ clothing items at Fashion

Week in New York City. In the summer of 2011, Dr. Gaines flew to New York to tour various schools in areas such as Manhattan and Long Island. She is currently collaborating with one of the superintendents in New York to bring Bus-stop 2 Bus-stop™ fashions into schools as a cultural and academic tool.

"I definitely think that educational clothes are ground-breaking styles that will change not only fashion, but the current practices in education," Dr. Gaines concludes.

Academic Clothing and Accessories: Learning in Style

According to Dr. Gaines's belief number one, "Clothing worn to school by students, teachers, staff, and administrators should serve some educational purpose." In alignment with this belief, Dr. Gaines has created a clothing line that expands across many subject areas and grade levels. The first Bus-stop 2 Bus-stop™ clothing items were made by Dr. Gaines to wear and display at her dissertation defense. They included two women's suit coat jackets with multiplication facts embroidered on them. Dr. Gaines wore a yellow suit coat jacket with 6 x 7 = 42 embroidered on the back. Her additional suit coat jacket was pink with 8 x 4= 32 embroidered on the back. As part of her dissertation defense, she illustrated the purposes of clothing in various professions.

Purposes of Clothing in Various Professions

Medical Doctor	Firefighter	Military Soldier	School Teacher
Surgical mask- conceals bacteria	Protective goggles- protects eyes	Steel-toed Boots- protects feet	Casual Shirts? ?
White lab coat- Scientific authority	Fire-proof suit- Protects skin	Camouflage clothing- Disguises soldier	Casual Dress/ Pants? ?

Medical doctors, firefighters, and military personnel wear clothing that reflect their overall career goal. The Bus-stop 2 Bus-stop™ method includes re-designing school staff and student clothing to reflect the school's overall goal, which is to increase student achievement. Students, teachers, and staff should wear clothing with academic content on the exterior of the clothing. Also, student uniforms should have multiplication facts, polygons, types of lines and angles, and other academic content to be learned by visual learning, social learning, and repetition.

School Uniforms: A Touchy Subject

There are mixed feelings about the wearing of school uniforms. Uniforms are intended to create a standardized dress and appearance of togetherness and/or equality. Also, uniforms create a less judgmental atmosphere since all students wear similar or identical clothing regardless of race, class, or gender. However, some students, parents, and others dislike the use of school uniforms because it takes away the student's individual expression. Others argue that uniforms falsely represent the diversity of real-life society.

In contrast, uniforms such as sports uniforms provide a specific function. Colors and patterns of teams provide a visual aid to distinguish each team. Likewise, school uniforms can present a learning opportunity. With Bus-stop 2 Bus-stop™ educational uniforms and clothing, students can wear school uniforms with academic content to create style and enhance school culture.

A Low-Cost Educational Clothing Alternative

A cost effective alternative for schools with low budgets is to use embroidery, adhesive tags, or pin-on tags. Visitors should have academic content on their name tags. Cafeteria staff, janitorial staff, crossing guards, and maintenance crews should wear clothing with academic content also. This method of including academic content on clothing should include cheerleader uniforms, football jerseys, choir robes, and many other extra-curricular clothing. As role models, the school district and school administration personnel should also wear Bus-stop 2 Bus-stop™ clothing.

Testing Precautions and Other Concerns

Since Bus-stop 2 Bus-stop™ educational clothing features visual images of academic content, a plan should be created for district, state, and national testing. This educational clothing will need to be covered for the entire time-span of the testing. A solution is for students to wear a regular school uniform or a temporary covering during any type of testing.

With new assessments such as the "Common Core Standards," students are tested on a higher Depth of Knowledge (DOK) level. Although Bus-stop 2 Bus-stop™ educational clothing features basic concepts, the students will still have to apply them to answer a test question correctly. The following example shows an educational clothing item and one corresponding standardized test-type multiple choice question. As shown below, the student is still required to read (or listen) and apply his or her knowledge to answer the question.

Bus-stop 2 Bus-stop™ Clothing Example	Example Test Question
	1. What shape has 4 sides of equal length and 4 corners? A. Triangle B. Rectangle C. Square D. None of the above

Chapter 7 Research Focus: Clothing and Society

Clothing plays an important part in American culture. Evidence from the earliest human civilizations proves the significance of clothing types. Factors such as climate, careers, religious beliefs, and geographical locations play a very large role in the physical appearance of certain clothing choices. The fabric, color, and style of a specific type of clothing often relates to one (or more) of the above factors. In America, the fashion industry is influenced by popular culture and forms of media. Modern trends sometimes stem from historical styles. American subcultures will take certain trends and eventually transform them into a lifestyle of specific clothing, as with sports uniforms. For example, ethnic clothing can tie into specific beliefs, religious values, or customs. Overall, global societies illustrate depth and diversity of clothing types in the world.

Clothing can be used to define a person's lifestyle and beliefs. Although the clothing worn may not reflect the person's individuality, it serves as a guide to initially judge a person. American society, through media and culture, has defined clothing types. Business wear, casual wear, swimwear, school uniforms, etc. can be used to identify, criticize, and categorize a person. Unlike cars, phones, or type of house, clothing criticism is usually taken very personally by the individual. Research points out a positive correlation between personal identity and clothing. Clothing is also capable of expressing personal thoughts and feelings. However, the interpretation of the clothing's visual appearance is up to a person's individual perception.

Many factors influence modern fashion today. The media and popular culture often influence new clothing fads and trends. Also, a person's environment and surroundings play a large role in influencing clothing styles and perceptions. Wealthy, middle class, and low class all differ in their perception of clothing types. For example, "wealthy" people do not consider cost, while "middle class" people wear clothing to satisfy the basic human need of warmth and protection, while still taking into account cost versus perception. Also, the weather affects a person's clothing. In fact, cold and snowy areas and hot tropical areas concentrate on their specific type of clothing to be marketed and sold in that area.

Discussion Questions for Chapter 7

1. Do you think Bus-stop 2 Bus-stop™ educational clothing methods will be more successful with students who wear uniforms or with students who wear casual clothing?
2. How will Bus-stop 2 Bus-stop™ clothing change fashion trends in America?
3. In your opinion, will American students embrace Bus-stop 2 Bus-stop™ educational clothing more or less than other countries? Why?
4. In your opinion, what are the two main clothing items that will be most popular for youth and teens?
5. According to the Chapter 7 research focus, what factors affect the physical appearance of clothing items?

Bus-stop 2 Bus-stop™ Journal Activity

Create a t-shirt that displays academic content on the front. For this activity, create the t-shirt in a manner that will interest elementary children. Write about your educational t-shirt and describe its appearance.

CHAPTER 8

Bus-stop 2 Bus-stop™ by 2020: Political, Legal, and Ethical Concerns

Consider this: "If teachers (salespersons) are required to "sell education" (sell products) just as businesses do, most of our schools (businesses) will be unsuccessful (go out of business) because students (customers) are not self-motivated (not willing to buy) the lesson (products)"

—Keshia L. Gaines, Ph.D.

Why is Dr. Gaines the first to create Bus-stop 2 Bus-stop™?

It would seem like the Bus-stop 2 Bus-stop™ method would have been created, implemented, and used in public schools a long, long time ago. After the U.S. released "A Nation at Risk" in 1983, American public schools were considered at-risk for future failure. At that point, authorities should have considered drastically re-structuring public schools. Why did American school authorities decide to continue the same unsuccessful in-classroom practices without trying new out-of-the-classroom areas for learning?

Furthermore, mathematics and science achievement in America has steadily declined over the last two decades. National, state, and local school authorities have realized that solely learning inside the classroom is not working effectively. With technology and the Internet being updated at a fast-changing pace, school districts must keep up with current trends. Schools should consider these updates and how to use this updated technology with the Bus-stop 2 Bus-stop™ method.

The Politics Behind American Schools

Behind the scenes, a range of political and social problems add to the national school failure epidemic. Some people blame incompetent teachers, while others blame the lack of funding for education and society's nonchalant attitude about learning. Many school practitioners today agree that American public schools are fighting a losing battle.

Often, teachers receive little or no support from parents or community members. American students continue to not meet the standards for reading, writing, and mathematics. Elementary students, as young as kindergarten and 1st grade, are being retained, attending summer school, or simply passed on to the next grade without mastering the content.

Education, at any level, is an important part of the lives of every American student. To ensure future success, specific changes should be made within the school setting. The staffing and personnel structure is essential for the school to be successful; this area could benefit from organizational change. In fact, there are several areas that should undergo organizational change to increase a school's successfulness. According to the author, the following areas within school systems could benefit from organizational change:

1. administration of public schools
2. teaching methods of general and special education students
3. specific duties of classified (and certified) personnel

Legal Aspects of American Schools

The current educational system in the U.S. can be improved with a few changes from legislation and higher authorities in education. Many lawmakers do not have an understanding of the true need for change because they do not work directly with public school students in the public school setting. Currently, the public education system is failing at its goals, and society is changing for the worse.

Teen pregnancy, dropout rates, and school violence are introduced and sometimes promoted in society and then brought into the classroom. This poses a problem for many school employees because they cannot solely focus on the academic goals of the school and school district. In many cases, policies and educational laws restrict educators from addressing controversial issues and student concerns.

First of all, the structure and effectiveness of the administration in many public K-12 schools is a big concern. In almost all school districts, there are many high-salaried persons who work in the central office of the school district. Although some of these positions are necessary, some can be consolidated so that additional funds could be available for hiring teachers, teacher assistants, and others that could work directly with students. In critical need areas (geographical and subject areas) there is a great shortage of teachers, even though there is not a significant problem with staffing administrators. Even though the national teacher shortage is recognized, the problem still exists. If administrators do not have quality teachers to staff the classrooms, then the school will not be successful.

After quantity of teachers, comes quality of teachers. In the human resources department, job vacancy advertising is a lengthy process that may include typing job descriptions, running ads in local media, sending out application packets to prospective job-seekers, etc. If a particular job is not filled, the classroom might have a permanent substitute, a non-qualified teacher, or classes that are over-crowded due to the teacher shortage. This teacher shortage situation concerns stakeholders because the students may not be getting the best possible education that they could receive.

Teacher Pancakes: High Turn-over Rates

Some schools have problems with high teacher turn-over rates. Geographical location may in fact play a part in this turnover because of harsh surroundings, crime, and lack of teacher resources. Often times, nearby universities provide a substantial amount of applicants to fill the positions that are vacant. Some education critics blame low teacher salaries as the reason for not attracting a good quantity and quality of teachers. On average, teacher salaries are lower than other careers which require a four-year college degree. Many teachers with less than five years of teaching experience leave the teaching field and begin working in a less stressful and higher paying job position.

Special Education: Special Concerns

The next concern is the special education system and the hiring of special education personnel. Currently, special education makes up one of the largest teacher shortage areas. Even though laws such as The No Child Left Behind Act of 2001 came about to nationally push for accountability of teachers and schools, there continues to be a problem with staffing special education and inclusion classrooms. Some public schools serve low to low-middle income students and have a high number of special education students.

In areas with predominately African-American students and other minorities, there is also a shortage of African American male teachers. This is a major concern since African-American male students make up the highest demographic of special education in some cases. Research pinpoints this as one reason why African American males do not return to the classroom as school teachers. Also, The No Child Left Behind Act of 2001 and other special education mandates have added extra responsibilities to general education and special education teachers.

Human resources and administration departments are handling the management of support personnel. Bus drivers, cafeteria workers, janitors, etc. all play an important role in the daily operation of a school. There is sometimes a shortage of support personnel because of low salaries. Even though some support personnel get school insurance packages, maybe if salaries were raised, schools would be able to hire and retain a great amount of qualified support personnel. Once successful hiring is done, then a staff development program can be implemented to help them succeed.

School Administrators Set the Tone

The *Statement of Ethics for School Administrators* is an ethics guide that was published by the American Association of School Administrators to provide guidance in the work place. In short, all administrators should take into consideration the ethical responsibilities of themselves and their employees. An administrator whom implements the Bus-stop 2 Bus-stop™ method into his or her school should consider all ethical aspects of the school setting with the well-being of the students in mind. Administrators, as well as other school personnel should follow all local, state, and national laws within the school setting. Also, he or she should ensure that all of their employees are aware of the ethical policies by giving professional development opportunities and training sessions.

School administrators should be educational leaders who promote the success of all students. Today's administrators have to adapt to the learning environment and culture of the students in the school. Many classrooms are diverse, especially inclusion settings, so administrators have to assist their teachers and help students be successful. School administrators should promote the success of all students by having a school culture and instructional program conducive to student learning and staff professional growth. All students should have an equal opportunity to learn in the classroom as well as outside the classroom.

There are concerns that some school cultures are not friendly enough to support the various learning styles of students. In the inclusion classroom, for example, there are pros and cons of having both special needs students and general education students in the same classroom (see Chapter 8 Research Focus: Ability Grouping and Student Tracking Methods). One benefit is that both special needs and general education students will not be subject to separation because they have different learning styles and/or abilities. This gives every student an equal opportunity to learn the same academic content. It also does not exclude special education students from learning general education content. Also, special education students can receive peer tutoring from general education students. A school administrator should oversee and analyze the school's environment to make sure that all students are treated fairly. Certain students, such as special education students, could be subject to teasing and negative peer pressure from others.

The school administrator should take into account the stakeholder's (community member's) visions for the school and the future of the students in their community. Stakeholders are very important in the decision-making process of school issues. They can include parents, community members, businesses, etc. Their input is very critical for school administrators to analyze the values of the community and compare them with the values within the school.

In conclusion, school administrators and other personnel should act with integrity, fairness, and in an ethical manner while implementing the Bus-stop 2 Bus-stop™ method. This is very important because a teacher or administrator cannot be consistent with school policies and procedures if they do not treat all students, parents, and stakeholders with fairness. The district should also aid the students, teachers, and administrators with the learning and understanding of the educational and organizational vision of the school and how it relates to their idea of integrity within the system. The school district should provide a full range of educational and developmental services to all stakeholders to promote community involvement. With the issue of fairness, the school district must provide a level of quality services to all stakeholders regardless of personal information such as age, race, religion, disability, or ability to pay for services. In addition to the school administrator, educators must understand the political, social, economic, legal, and cultural context of learning and the school environment. The ability to "re-frame" thoughts to see different viewpoints is critical to a career in education.

Overall success in school districts includes each faculty and staff member working towards goals to benefit students.

Schools should provide a variety of services for students, parents, and stakeholders to make the educational process a success. These services may include after-school programming, teacher and administrative training, curriculum development, school improvement, professional development, and other forms of school improvement.

What do schools need to be successful with Bus-stop 2 Bus-stop™?

1. Clear educational goals and/or a mission statement
2. Policies and procedures that embrace the "Bus-stop 2 Bus-stop™" culture
3. Adaptation of this method to student's needs
4. High expectations for all students
5. Administer routine assessment
6. Provide multiple opportunities for Bus-stop 2 Bus-stop™ learning during the school day
7. Consider politics, ethics, and student safety while implementing this learning method
8. Make the Bus-stop 2 Bus-stop™ method relevant to students

Chapter 8 Research Focus: Ability Grouping and Student Tracking Methods

One issue facing schools today is the performance rate of various students. Some students are separated by ability groups, which is a type of grouping based on a student's academic performance. Although ability grouping students can provoke negative issues, they also have some positive benefits. Test scores are used to determine the ability of learners, and those of the same proficiency are grouped together. Students begin to associate with those from their groups during classes.

Ability grouping was started in primary schools in the United Kingdom, but later was so popular that it became the main organizational form in both primary and secondary schools (Ireson & Hallam, 2001). To be able to understand the meaning of ability grouping, there is a need to understand the various types of ability groupings that exist. According to Sears and Sorensen (2001), there are four types of ability grouping: setting, streaming, mixed ability, and within-class grouping. Streaming, setting, and within-class groupings are mostly used by teachers to reduce diversity among learners. Pupils of the same ability are classed together although mixed ability groupings encourage diversity. In this case, students are grouped according to their previous academic performance in the classroom and on academic assessments.

Ability grouping has various effects on students. Ability groups are advantageous to the students because groups give them an opportunity to be instructed at different paces. There exist differences in academic performance between students, so their learning pace may be different. High ability learners learn concepts very fast compared to the low ability students (Slavin, 1996). Slavin (1996) continues to argue that the problem of instructional pace among learners is solved by these groups as learners of the same ability are grouped together. This enables them to grasp concepts at the same time. When learners are grouped by ability, the low ability learners find it easy to engage in learning without fear of criticism from higher-performing peers. The low ability students feel inferior to the high ability students and this may hinder student participation in class work. In ability groups, all learners have a better chance of getting the instructor's attention. This is because in mixed ability groups, teachers sometimes concentrate more on the high performers at the expense of other students.

Ability grouping also has a negative impact on the low ability learners in that it badly affects their self-esteem, self-confidence, and their attitudes towards school and schoolwork (Ireson & Hallam, 2001). Low ability students feel embarrassed and this might adversely affect their self-esteem as they go on with school years. The placement of students in different classes is a constant reminder of their performance in class and this makes the low performers feel inferior to their high ability counterparts. This could end up affecting them in other aspects of life. Students who are constantly in the lower groups are most likely to view themselves as inferior and this might lead to them having a negative attitude towards school and school work. Further, it could lead to school drop-outs by the low ability students or animosity among students. The low ability group may feel inferior the high ability group, which could possibly bring about serious divisions within the school.

Also, the self-image of learners is greatly affected by ability groups. Low ability students have lower self-esteem as compared to the high ability students and this results in serious effects among the students of different groups (Sears & Sorensen, 2001). Teacher's attitudes are also a great way to determine the way students look at themselves. Students look to teachers as their role models. Therefore, any form of criticism from the teachers is taken seriously by the students. Some teachers tend to favor the high ability students more than those of low ability; this makes these students devalue themselves. The behavior of teachers towards these students may drive them from school and such students could end up involved in negative behaviors as a way of settling their disappointments. Ireson and Hallam (2001) argue that the perception of low ability students is greatly influenced by the teachers' behavior and attitudes towards them. There have been various propositions for equal treatment of students by teachers regardless of their academic ability and level; it will ensure there is no lack of self-esteem and bad self-image among students (Bryson & Bentley, 1980).

The question of ability groups increasing learning has been greatly debated by scholars. Some feel that it is advantageous and helps students learn while others argue that it is detrimental to learning. According to Wheelock (1994), ability groups do not promote student learning and they hinder the academic achievement of all student levels. Wheelock then proposes alternatives to ability groups and states the purpose for the need to use these alternatives in elementary school. Alternatives to ability groups are also suggested by Slavin (1996) since it is the only way teachers in elementary school can avoid making decisions that could end up causing negative effects on the students' self-esteem. Alternatives to ability groups include cooperative and mastery learning. Mastery learning involves the teaching of several lessons and then testing the understanding of the concept taught on the learners. Those found to have difficulties with the taught concept are given additional tutorials separately to make sure they understand. Cooperative learning refers to a method of instruction in which learners are grouped into small groups of mixed abilities and taught from these groups.

According to Sears and Sorensen (2001), ability groups do not help student learning since these groupings are not always done objectively and they are sometimes inconsistent. Ability groups should allow student mobility from one ability group to another, and therefore requires a good system to regularly check student performance on tests. Very few schools have effective systems of this nature, so some groups are not effectively checked. As a result, student learning is weakened by the ability groups rather than strengthened. Other studies argue that ability grouping significantly helps students to learn. Students in the higher ability groups are found to learn more and attain higher achievement, but the lower groups students achieve very little (Blau, 2004).

The topic on ability groups has attracted controversy among different scholars. Some agree with ability grouping and some argue against its application in elementary schools. Ability grouping has been found to be very beneficial to high ability group students but detrimental to low ability students. The supporters of ability groups argue that if adjustments are made on the method of grouping, then ability groups would be an effective method to increase achievement among students. Those opposed to ability groupings, however, suggest several alternatives to it that are less detrimental and do not affect students negatively (Blau, 2004). There is a need for teachers to carefully analyze the various types of ability groups and choose the one that is most appropriate for their students, because certain learning strategies are effective for a certain audiences.

In conclusion—Remember the political, legal, and ethical aspects of the Bus-stop 2 Bus-stop™ method.

Money, money, money . . . and more money!

In a perfect world, a school district could spend millions on researching and implementing the Bus-stop 2 Bus-stop™ method. However, in the recent U.S. economic recession, many school budgets have been greatly reduced. How can schools with low or no funds allocated to school improvement implement the Bus-stop 2 Bus-stop™ method?

Write a grant to use this method in your school!

The Bus-stop 2 Bus-stop™ method can be used to improve your school! Search for school improvement grants on the internet to fund this learning method. Also, a school in need of funding can create fundraisers or ask for donations from school sponsors.

Remember, Safety First

Please consider the political, legal, and social aspects of Bus-stop 2 Bus-stop™. Keep safety in mind and use these methods carefully and safely. Do not place Bus-stop 2 Bus-stop™ academic content in places where it will block safety exits, fire extinguishers, or other important areas.

A successful administrator knows how to balance principal responsibilities while maintaining a safe, orderly school. A school administrator should ensure that management of the organization creates a safe, efficient, and effective learning environment. A school administrator should know how to coordinate a system of delegation and faculty-staff evaluations to ensure school success.

Discussion Questions for Chapter 8

1. What are some important safety concerns that schools must discuss before the Bus-stop 2 Bus-stop™ method is implemented?
2. Why should teacher lesson plans and Bus-stop 2 Bus-stop™ learning areas have the same overall educational goal?
3. In your opinion, how does politics within a school affect the Bus- stop 2 Bus-stop™ learning method?
4. What are some politics behind American schools that may contribute to educational failure?
5. What are two negative and two positive aspects of student ability grouping?

Bus-stop 2 Bus-stop™ Journal Activity

Write a mini-grant for funds to implement the Bus-stop 2 Bus-stop™ learning method at a local school. What out-of-classroom areas and are most likely to get funded by a donor?

Conclusion

So . . . Why are students not learning on the school bus and other non-traditional areas outside the classroom?

Given the research findings and theories to aid in understanding failure of public schools in America, students should be learning academic content on the school bus. Actually, students should be learning academic content at the bus-stop, cafeteria, playground, bathrooms, video arcades, and other areas of the school. The responsibility of student success falls upon the teachers and school administrators. Collaboratively, school staff members can analyze their school culture and implement the Bus-stop 2 Bus-stop™ method based on individual student need. The future of education is looking much brighter with the Bus-stop 2 Bus-stop™ method of learning outside the classroom.

APPENDIX A

Additional Literature Review on Visual Learning

According to Benson (1997), the words of the great philosopher Aristotle are true; thinking is made possible by images. Benson (1997) maintains that this has played an important role in the shaping of education, especially in the contemporary society. Nevertheless, Benson (1997) concludes that there still are a lot of teachers who are either unaware or unwilling to promote visual learning tools in their classrooms. This is seen particularly with language teachers, who seem to focus too much on the spoken or written word.

According to Paivio (1991), the cognitive process, in general, consists of interplay of both visual and verbal elements. The use of both elements is the key to information processing. This has particularly gained recognition from individuals who make use of multimedia in education. Mayer & Sims (1994) suggests that as childhood educators get more enlightened on the significance of visual learning aids, they incorporate them to help their young students. Educators across the world are recognizing the need for effective and appropriate employment of visual learning aids with students of all levels. Mayer & Sims (1994) further argues that as student's get older, their ability to learn through visual aids gets better and more visual learning aids can be incorporated.

In Mayer (2001), there is a strong link existing between verbal and non-verbal codes. He understands verbal codes to mean verbal language that symbolizes both concrete and abstract experiences. The non-verbal codes are concerned more with non-linguistic language What?. This kind of information is of great importance in education because it describes how learning enables retention, manipulation, and transformation of the learning world either mentally or through imagination. The definition offered by Mayer (2001) of multimedia instructional messages (MIM) captures and actually sums up the whole idea of visual learning. He says that MIM is nothing more than presentations that encompass both pictures and words. Mayer understands images as referring to both dynamic and static graphics.

Paivio (1986) introduces an interesting understanding of visual learning. For him, visual and verbal systems, as two distinct levels of processing, can actually take place. In order to demonstrate this further, he offers the example of a cat. Whenever the word 'cat' is mentioned, the verbal memory code is activated at one level, and at another level the picture of a cat comes into action in the visual system. Paivio (1986) considers this representational processing. Further, he states that referential processing comes in after the representational processing, and serves to cross-activate the verbal and non-verbal codes. Continuing with the example of the cat, the mention of the word 'cat' necessarily invokes the visual system representation of the same, and the presentation of a picture of a cat automatically comes to mind. For that reason, Paivio (1991) considered visual aids as a necessary for learning, and states that learning would be totally impossible without them.

An additional thought regarding the interaction of the two systems is offered by Rieber (1994), who argues that verbal and visual do not always relate. He says this is because images have the ability to bring forth verbal labels. For that reason, he brings in the idea of associative processing, where additional information is activated within each of the systems. He says that there are several instances where visual information is transformed into verbal forms and stored in the long term memory (Rieber, 1994). He further states that linguistic representation is better generated in students who made use of graphic organizers compared to those who used other methods of learning. For this reason, learning should be designed in a way that makes it possible for these different processing methods to interact.

Mayer and Sims (1994), argues that in order to reap the most out of learning activities, educators should incorporate joint usage of visual and verbal aids. The popular adage that pictures are worth thousands of words support the understanding of why visual-verbal language is central to efficient communication and learning. Many theorists (Mayer 2001, and Chandler & Sweller, 1991) have indicated that students make use of 'stand-alone' diagrams that are visual-verbal integrated; studies have shown an increase in performance from about 23 percent to about 90 percent. Stand-alone diagrams are considered as those which possess all the elements and verbal basics that are needed for full understanding without necessitating other texts from elsewhere.

Diagrams, charts, and maps are very common tools in the process of visual learning. In a research on the effects specific visual skills had on learning, Kleinman and Dwyer (1999) established that color graphics provided better tools for study and were better understood than graphics presented in black and white. A study that was earlier conducted by Heinich et al. (1999) also agreed with that of Kleinman and Dwyer (1999) that color graphics were better than black and white. However, Heinich et al. (1999) found no significant difference in the overall achieved learning.

While studying the effects of film subtitles in a second language, Danan (1992) agreed that it had an effect on improving vocabulary. This study was done within the context of dual coding theory, due to its effect on both visual and verbal systems. According to Doyle (1999), visual organizers are rooted in the schema theory. This simply refers to inter-linked nature of knowledge, both new and old. In other words, when new knowledge is acquired, it must be linked with the already existing knowledge for learning to take place. As stated by Doyle (1999) teachers have the duty of presenting materials in such a way that students are able to link the knowledge they already possess to the new knowledge. This leads the students to develop their own schema, which is necessary for understanding the concepts. The emphasis here is on the significance of prior knowledge activation in the learning process. Comprehension according to What is SCHEMA???? Campbell and Stanley (1993) is possible only where interaction between old and new knowledge takes place.

According to theorists (Mayer and Sims, 1994; Paivio, 1986, and Benson, 1997), the amount of mental resources required to process any kind of information is referred to as cognitive load. This theory claims that only so much information can be acquired by the working memory at one time, and that any attempt to go beyond that limit would lead to loss of the information. Quite a number of researchers (Mayer 2001; Danan, 1992, and Chandler and Sweller, 1991) have agreed that instructional design can greatly benefit from the use of visual learning tools for the reduction of the cognitive load. They recognize a number of instructional strategies and their impact on the cognitive load. The two strategies are called modality effect and split attention effect. These strategies were found to have the impact of reducing the cognitive load. In one study, geometry students advanced in achievement when visual diagrams were accompanied by audio explanations. In the same study, it was found that with diverse information sources students were unable to deeply process information due to working memory overload (Paivio, 1991). A study by Horn (1998) established that the format of presentation of study content affected the reasoning abilities of students. Students that used pictorial materials were recorded with better reaction times, as well as a greater understanding.

According to a quasi-experimental study conducted by Brookbank et al. (1999) vocabulary skills of both elementary and junior high school students had been improved by the application of graphic organizers. This study was conducted with the assistance of teachers who were preparing for their masters dissertations over a period of 16 weeks. Over this period, the teachers introduced their students to various visual organizers and instructed them on how to understand and clarify concepts; demonstrate details, ideas, as well as their relation; how to make analogies; and how to show order and sequences. In order to monitor the differences, Brookbank et al (1999) used pre and post-observational checklists. They established that over 80 percent of students at every level were enabled to develop a mastery of vocabulary.

Brookbank et al. (1999) and Sinatra et al. (1984) carried out research on the effects of the use of visual organizers for the improvement of reading comprehension for grades 2 through 8 with learning disabled students. During one of the researches (Sinatra et al., 1984), a pre-reading strategy was employed, where mapping was used and compared to the approach of verbal readiness. This twenty-seven student study attempted to improve comprehension in reading. After the tests, the scores revealed that those students who used the approach of mapping had higher academic achievement than students using verbal readiness.

A further research conducted by Brookbank et al (1999) with the same intention as that of Sinatra et al. (1984), revealed that the students generally made remarkable gains on the tests taken. This study was of students in the first, second, fifth, and seventh grades. Brookbank et al. (1999) and Sinatra et al. (1984) discovered that semantic mapping was actually an extremely useful way of enhancing learning. In particular, they recorded benefits in the following areas for both students and teachers:

1. Students are encouraged and motivated to reflect on and track their reading.
2. Students are also enabled to develop summaries that are visually coherent.
3. Teachers are able to come up with reading lessons that are more focused and purposeful.

4. Visual organizers also provided a structure on the basis of which pre-reading experiences are guided.
5. Teachers are enabled to organize the effort of readers toward pre-determined comprehension objectives.

A study by Troyer (1994), established that graphic organizers provided a much better strategy for effective comprehension reading as compared to others such as question-answer or mental models. Basically, Troyer (1994) found that more students were at home with the use of visual organizers for learning than with other methods, such as kinesthetic or audio. The reason why his study is considered significant is that it involved more than 173 students of various grade levels. Students were classified on the basis of three conditions: control read/answer, graphic organizer, and mental modeling groups. In each of the groups, instructions were based on varying text organizational patterns, comparison, collection, and attribution. After the instructions, students in each of the groups were given tests, and students in the graphic organizer group advanced more than the other two groups.

Golon (2006) argues scientific evidence stands to prove that between 75 and 80 percent of the gifted individuals in society are visual-spatial learners. He further adds that in some of the schools that he was employed, over 98 percent of the students were actually visual-spatial learners, and over 90 percent of students who were placed in special education classes also fell in the category of visual-spatial learners. Golon (2006) also felt that out of the studies conducted in Arizona, over 80 percent were actually in the visual-spatial learners' category and preferred it. Nevertheless, he also noted with concern the gearing of schools towards left-hemispheric learning. Left-hemispheric learning takes one step at a time; therefore students are required to master an area before being allowed to move up the ladder of academics. He also noted that in the higher grades, teaching occurred in a strictly auditory fashion, unlike in the lower grades where hands-on learning was incorporated. This is a major concern, according to Ritchie and Volkl (2000), because visual aids such as graphs, maps, and posters, help move students away from left hemispheric learning. Golon (2006) says that in most cases, whenever visual-spatial students are presented with introductory material for learning, they are often required to assimilate it in sequential fashion, which requires them to use their weaker (left) hemisphere. He says this can be compared to a person whose dominant arm is broken and forced to take notes with the weaker hand, and then blame them for a poor handwriting. Nevertheless, Gordon says that with continued practice, it is possible for that person to produce writing that is legible, but would never at any point attain the excellence of the dominant arm. Doyle (1999) agrees with this argument when he observes that almost every culture bears prejudices against the use of the left hand, which is directed by the right hemisphere of the mind. Silverman (2002) says that while the right hemisphere is acknowledged as being in charge of the regulation of attention functions of the brain, failure to activate and engage the right hemisphere leads to low attention and poor learning in students. Silverman (2002) introduces very interesting observations that whether a student uses the visual-spatial style or not, they must necessarily use the right hemispheres in order to learn.

REFERENCES

Al-Balhan, E.M. (2007). Learning Styles in Relation to Academic Performance in Middle School Mathematics, *Domes*, 16(1)

Alferink, L. A., & Farmer-Dougan, V. (2010). Brain-(not) based education: Dangers of misunderstanding and misapplication of neuroscience research. *Exceptionality*, 18(1), 42-52.

Anderson, R., & Shifrin, Z. (1980). *The Meaning of Words in Context*. Hillsdale, NJ: Lawrence Erlbaum Associates

Baker, D. P., Fabrega, R., Galindo, C., & Mishook, J. (2005). Instructional time and national achievement: Cross-national evidence. *Prospects* 34 (3).

Bender, N. W. & Larkin, J. M. (2009). *Reading strategies for elementary students with learning difficulties: strategies for RTI*. Thousand Oaks, CA: Corwin Press.

Benson, P. (1997). Problems in Picturing Text: A Study of Visual/Verbal Problem Solving. *Technical Communication Quarterly*, 6 (2) 141-160

Bergen, D. (2002). Evaluating 'brain-based' curricular claims. Social Education, 66(5), 376.Blakemore, C. L. (2003). Movement is essential to learning. *JOPERD—The Journal of Physical Education, Recreation & Dance*, 74(9), 22.

Blakemore, C. (2003). Movement is Essential to Learning. Journal of Physical Education, Recreation, & Dance, 74(9), 1-7.

Blau, J. R. (2004). *The Blackwell companion to sociology.* Malden, MA: Wiley-Blackwell

Bodrova, E., & Leong, D. (1996). Tools of the mind: the Vygotskian approach to early childhood education. Englewood Cliffs, N.J.: Merrill.

Boucher, A., & Wiseman, E. (2011). *Movement discovery: physical education for children.* Sudbury: Jones and Bartlett Publishers.

Bransford, J., Brown, A., & Cocking, R. (2000). *How People Learn: Brain, Mind, and Experience & School.* Washington, DC: National Academy Press.

Brookbank, D., Grover, S., Kullberg, K., & Strawser, C. (1999) *Improving Student Achievement Through Organization of Student Learning.* Chicago: Saint Xavier University and IRI/Skylight

Brophy, E. J. (2010). *Motivating students to learn.* New York: Routledge.

Bruer, J. T. (1997a). A science of learning. *The American School Board Journal, 184(2),* 24-27.

Bruer, J. T. (1997b). Education and the brain: A bridge too far. *Educational Researcher,* 26 (8), 4-16.

Bryson, J. E., & Bentley, C. P. (1980). *Ability grouping of public school students: legal aspects of classification and tracking methods.* Charlottesville, VA: Michie Co.

Bucko, R. L. (1997). Brain basics: Cognitive psychology and its implications for education. *ERS Spectrum, 15(3),* 20-25.

Caine, R. N., & Caine, G. (1990). Understanding a brain-based approach to learning and teaching. *Educational Leadership, 48(2),* 66-70.

Caine, R. N., & Caine, G. (1994). *Making connections: Teaching and the human brain.* Menlow Park, CA: Addison Wesley Longman.

Campbell, D. & Stanley, J. (1993). *Experimental and Quasi-Experimental Designs for Research.* Boston: Houghton Mifflin Company

Carroll, J. B. (1963). *The study of language: a survey of linguistics and related disciplines in America.* Cambridge: Harvard University Press.

Chance, P. (2001, September-October). Becoming a 'wiz' at brain-based teaching: From translation to application. *Psychology Today,* 34(5), 72.

Chandler, P. & Sweller, J. (1991). Cognitive Load Theory and the Format of Instruction. *Cognition and Instruction,* 8 (4) 293-332

Chang, K., Chen, I., & Sung, Y. (2002). The effect of concept mapping to enhance text comprehension and summarization. *The Journal of Experimental Education* 71(1), 5-23.

Danan, M. (1992). Reversed Subtitling and Dual Coding Theory: New Directions for Foreign Language Instruction. *Language Learning,* 42, 497-527

Daniels, H. (2001). *Vygotsky and pedagogy.* London: Routledge-Falmer.

Davis, S. M. (2000). Look before you leap: Concerns about 'brain-based' products and approaches. *Childhood Education,* 77(2), 100.

Denham, C. (1980). Time to learn: a review of the Beginning Teacher Evaluation Study, conducted with funds provided by the National Institute of Education. Sacramento, Calif.: California Commission for Teacher Preparation and Licensing.

Dolya, G. (2010). *Vygotsky in action in the early years: the 'key to learning' curriculum.* London: Routledge.

Doyle, C. S. (1999). *The use of graphic organizers to improve comprehension of learning disabled students in social studie*s. Union, NJ: M. A. Research Project, Kean University. (ERIC Document Reproduction Service No. ED427313)

Dunn, R., & Griggs, S. A. (2000). Practical approaches to using learning styles in higher education. Westport, CT: Bergin and Garvey.

Fisher, D. (2009). The use of instructional time in the typical high school classroom. *The Educational Forum, 73*(2).

Gallick-Jackson, S. A. (1997) *Improving Narrative Writing Skills, Composition Skills, and Related Attitudes among Second Grade Students by Integrating Word Processing Graphic Organizers and Art into a Process Approach to Writing.* Fort Lauderdale, FL: Nova Southern University

Gatewood, T. E. (1989). Caution! Applying brain research to education. *The Clearing House, 63(1),* 37-39.

Gettinger, M. Seibert, J. K. (n.d). Best Practices in Increasing: Academic Learning Time, *Best Practices in School Psychology.* Retrieved on June 19, 2011 from http://www.aea1.k12.ia.us/docs/gettinger.pdf

Glickman, C.D., Gordon, S.P. & Ross—Gordon, J. M. (2010). *Supervision and Instructional Leadership: A Developmental Approach.* Boston: Pearson Education, Inc.

Goldberg, S. H. (2011). *Can The National Center on Time & Learning Bring Longer Schools Days to One Million Students?* Retrieved on June 20, 2011 from http://www. philasocialinnovations.org/site/index.php?option=com_ content&view=article&id=268:can-the-national-center-on-time-a-learning-bring-longer-schools-days-to-one-million-students-&catid=19:disruptive-innovations&Itemid=30

Golon, A.S. (2006). *The Visual-spatial Classroom: Differentiation that Engages Every Learner.* Denver, CO: Visual-Spatial Resource

Greenspan, S.I., (2000). The Irreducible Needs of Children: What Every Child Must have to Grow, Learn, and Flourish. Perseus Books.

Greenwood, C. S. (2010). *The power of words: learning vocabulary in grades 4-9.* Lanham, Md.: Rowman & Littlefield Education.

Hartman, H. (2002). Scaffolding & Cooperative Learning. *Human Learning and Instruction* (pp. 23-69). New York: City College of City University of New York.

Hedegaard, M. (2001). Learning in classrooms: a cultural-historical approach. Aarhus [u.a.: Aarhus Univ. Press

Heinich, R., Molenda, M., Russell, J., & Smaldino, S. (1999). Instructional Media and Technologies for Learning. (6th ed). (pp. 14-15, 21, 213-214, 290-291, 319-324). Upper Saddle River, New Jersey: Prentice-Hall.

Herbert, B. (2009, November 28). Stacking the Deck Against Kids. New York Times, p. A19.

Horn, R. (1998). *Mapping Great Debates: Can Computers Think?* Macro VU Press

Hruby, G. G. (1999). Teaching with the brain in mind. *Roeper Review*, 21(4), 326.

Huyvaert, S. H. (1998). *Time is of the essence: learning in schools.* Boston: Allyn and Bacon.

Hyerle, D. (1996). *Visual tools for constructing knowledge.* Alexandria, Va.: Association for Supervision and Curriculum Development.

Ireson, J., & Hallam S. (2001). *Ability grouping in education.* London, UK: SAGE

Jensen, E., & Dabney, M. W. (2000). *Learning smarter: the new science of teaching.* San Diego, CA: Brain Store.

Jensen, E. (1996). *Brain-based learning.* Del Mar, CA: Turning Point Publishing.

Jensen, E. (2008). *Brain-based learning: the new paradigm of teaching* (2nd ed.). Thousand Oaks, CA.: Corwin Press.

Jones, R. (1995). Smart brains. *The American School Board Journal, 182(11),* 22-26.

Jonson, F. K., Cappelloni, N., & Niesyn, M. (2011). *The new elementary teacher's handbook: flourishing in your first year.* Thousand Oaks, CA: Corwin.

Jorgenson, O. (2003). Brain scam? Why educators should be careful about embracing brain research. *The Educational Forum, 67(4),* 364-369.

Jowett, G. & Linton, J. (1989). *Movies as Mass Communication.* New York: Sage Publishers

Kirkland, L. D., Camp, D. & Manning, M. (2008). Changing the Face of Summer Programs *Childhood Education, 85(2)*

Kleinman, E. & Dwyer, F. (1999). Analysis of Computerized Visual Skills: Relationships to Intellectual Skills and Achievement. *International Journal of Instructional Media,* 26 (1) 53-69

Kosanovich, M.L., and Weinstein, C. & Goldman, E. (2009). *Using student center activities to differentiate instruction. A guide for teachers.* Portsmouth, NH: RMC Research Corporation, Center on Instruction

Lamb, M.E. (2005). Attachments, social networks, and developmental contexts. Human Development, 48: 108-112.

Levine, M. & Barringer, M. (2008). Brain-Based Research Helps to Identify and Treat Slow Learners. *Education Digest: Essential Readings Condensed for Quick Review,* 73(9), 9-13. Retrieved on June 21, 2011 from EBSCO*host.*

Lindsey, G. (1998-1999). Brain research and implications for early childhood education. *Childhood Education, 75(2),* 97-100.

Lombardi, J. (2008). Beyond learning styles: Brain-based research and English Language Learners. Heldref Publications. p.219

Marsick, J. V. & Watkins, E. K. (1990). *Informal and incidental learning in the workplace.* New York: Routledge.

Mayer, R. & Sims, V. (1994). For whom is a Picture worth a Thousand Words? Extensions of a Dual-coding Theory of Multimedia Learning. *Journal of Educational Technology,* 86, 389-401

Mayer, R. (2001). *Multimedia Learning.* Cambridge University Press

McKenzie, J. (1999). Scaffolding for Success. [Electronic version] *Beyond Technology, Questioning, Research and the Information Literate School Community.* Retrieved June 12, 2011, from http://fno.org/dec99/scaffold.html

McMurrer, J. (2008). *Instructional time in elementary schools: A closer look at changes for specific subjects. In From the*

capital to the classroom: Year of the No Child Left Behind Act. Washington, DC: Center on Education Policy.

Morgan, H. (1999). *The imagination of early childhood education.* Westport, CT: Bergin & Garvey.

Ngeow, K.K., &Yoon, S. (2001, October). Learning to learn: preparing teachers and students for problem-based learning. *ERIC Digest.* Retrieved June 20, 2011, from http://www.ed.gov/databases/ERIC_Digests/ed457524.html

Nystrand, M., & Gamoran, A. (1991). Student engagement: When recitation becomes conversation. In H. Waxman and H. Walberg (Eds.), *Contemporary Research on Teaching.* Berkeley: McCutchan. (A. Gamoran, second author).

Olson, J. and Pratt, J. (2000). The Instructional Cycle. *Teaching Children and Adolescents with Special Needs* (pp. 170-197). Upper Saddle River, NJ: Prentice-Hall, Inc.

O'Neil, J. & Marsick, J. V. (2007). *Understanding action learning.* New York: American Management Association.

Paivio, A. (1986). *Mental Representations: Dual-coding Approaches.* New York: Oxford University Press

Paivio, A. (1991). Dual-coding Theory: Retrospect and Current Status. *Canadian Journal of Psychology,* 45, 255-287

Phelps, M. (2010). Real-time Teaching and Learning. *Kappa Delta Pi Record,* 46(1)

Phillips, D. C. & Soltis, J. F. (1998). *Perspectives on learning* (3rd ed.). New York: Teachers College Press.

Pressley, M., Wharton-McDonald, R., Mistretta-Hampton, J.M., & Echevarria, M. (1998). The nature of literacy instruction in ten grade 4/5 classrooms in upstate New York. *Scientific Studies of Reading, 2,* 159-194.

Prigge, D.J. (2002). 20 ways to promote brain-based teaching and learning. *Intervention in School and Clinic, 37(4),* 237-241.

Raymond, E. (2000). Cognitive Characteristics. *Learners with Mild Disabilities* (pp. 169-201). Needham Heights, MA: Allyn & Bacon, A Pearson Education Company.

Reeves, D. B. (2004). *Accountability in action: a blueprint for learning organizations* (2nd ed.). Edgewood, CO: Advanced Learning Press

Rieber, L. (1994). *Computers, Graphics and Learning.* Madison, WI: WCB Brown and Benchmark

Ritchie, D. & Volkl, C. (2000). Effectiveness of two generative learning strategies in the science classroom. *School Science & Mathematics, 100*(2), 83-89.

Rock, M. L., & Thread, B. K. (2009). Promote student success during independent seatwork. *Intervention in School and Clinic,* 44(3).

Scales, P.C., Roehlkepartain, E.C., Neal, M., Kielsmeier, J.C. & Benson, P.L. (2006). Reducing Academic Achievement Gaps: the Role of Community Service and Service learning, The Journal of Experiential Education, 29(2)

Sears, J., & Sorensen, P. (2001). *Issues in science teaching.* New York, NY: Routledge

Silverman, L.K. (2002). *Upside-down Brilliance: The Visual-spatial Learner.* Denver, CO: Deleon Publishing

Simpson, D. (2006). The Impact of Breakfast Clubs on Pupil Attendance and Punctuality *Research in Education,* 6(2).

Sinatra, R. C., Stahl-Gemake, J., & Berg, D. N. (1984). Improving reading comprehension of disabled readers through semantic mapping. *Reading Teacher, 38*(1), 22-29.

Slavin, R. E. (1996). *Education for all.* New York, NY: Taylor & Francis

Sousa, D. A. (2003). *How the Gifted Brain Learns.* Thousand Oaks, CA: Corwin Press

Tripp, L., Basye, C., Jones, J. & Tripp, V. (2008). Teaching and Learning with Time Lines Social Education, 72(3)

Troyer, S. J. (1994, April) The effects of three instructional conditions in text structure on upper elementary students' reading comprehension and writing performance. Paper presented at the meeting of the American Educational Research Association, New Orleans, LA. (ERIC Document Service Reproduction No. ED 373315)

Vygotsky, L. S., & Cole, M. (1978). *Mind in society: the development of higher psychological processes.* Cambridge: Harvard University Press.

Vygotsky, L. S., & Hanfmann, E. (1967). *Thought and language* (3. pbk. print. ed.). Cambridge, Mass.: M.I.T. Press.

Wertsch, J. V. (1985). *Vygotsky and the social formation of mind.* Cambridge, Mass.: Harvard University Press.

Wheelock, A. (1994). *Alternatives to tracking and ability grouping.* Arlington, VA: American Association of School Administrators

Wolfe, P. (2001). *Brain matters: translating research into classroom practice.* Alexandria, VA: Association for Supervision and Curriculum Development.

Wood, Z. & Walker, J. (2007). Learning outside the Classroom: What Can Be Done in Lesson Time? *Teaching Geography,* 32 (3)

NOTES